BREAKING

LOOSE

TAKING YOUR MARRIAGE TO A HIGHER LEVEL OF FULFILLMENT

EBED
PUBLICATIONS
In love, serve one another

BY

NEIL RHODES

Breaking Loose

Copyright © 1997 by Neil Rhodes

ALL RIGHTS RESERVED

EBED Publications is a division of The McDougal Publishing Company, Hagerstown, Maryland.

Published by:

EBED Publications
P.O. Box 3595
Hagerstown, MD 21742-3595

ISBN 1-884369-57-X

Printed in the United States of America
For Worldwide Distribution

CONTENTS

DEDICATION

I dedicate this book to my "one-flesh" and lifelong partner in marriage and the Gospel, my ever-loving wife, Noline.

ACKNOWLEDGMENTS

Noline and I would like to acknowledge our very dear and best friends in the ministry, Mike and Marilyn Phillips, the head and international directors of Marriage Ministries International, for their love and unfailing stand for the healing of the home.

A very special thank you to our longtime friend and "spiritual mother," Elaine Van der Merwe. Elaine typed the original manuscript for us.

To Harold McDougal, our publisher and editor, thank you for your integrity and for the keen spiritual insight you gave to this book.

Foreword by Harold McDougal

No ministry is more important right now, anywhere in the world, than the ministry to married couples who are struggling to stay afloat in a sea of confusion, and I deeply appreciate and identify with those who have a burden for such ministry. If marriages continue to dissolve at the present rate, we are doomed to face coming generations of hurt and confused men and women and children.

Neil and Noline Rhodes have dedicated their lives to restoring health to the Christian marriage, and we take pleasure in publishing their second book on the subject. This one, like the first, is both honest and simple and looks to Christ as the source of strength for married couples today.

Since God is the author of the marriage plan, it behooves us all to look to Him for solutions to the present dilemma of selfishness and willfulness that is tearing marriages apart in record numbers. As the nation turns to God in a time of genuine repentance and revival, our prayer is that there will be, at the same time, a revival of truth concerning God's will for marriage and a willingness on the part of those who love Him to obey Him fully. And, since this book puts forth those ideals, may it be a blessing not only to Christian marriages across America, but around the world as well.

INTRODUCTION

Strong homes make strong churches; strong churches make strong communities; and strong communities make strong nations. From the very beginning, at the creation of Adam and Eve, God determined that the family would be the building block on which nations are formed. Because of this fact, it has always been the goal of Satan to break down the structure of the home and family. A family that is divided against itself cannot stand, and a downward spiral in the home and the gradual destruction of the family unit, if not quickly addressed, will eventually affect an entire nation.

Since the home is so vitally important to God, His heart is to provide salvation for the family as part of His total plan of redemption for mankind. We are redeemed from sin and death as individuals, we are blessed with healing and prosperity as individuals, and God wants this blessing to be for the family as a whole.

The most serious problem Christian married

couples are facing today is that the voices of the world are far too loud around us, and the voice of God far too muted. This is sad, for the world is confused, while God has genuine answers for the problems we face in our daily lives.

In fact, if we are willing to leave our preconceived ideas about marriage and allow God to teach us His ways, we can break loose from the chains that are preventing us from achieving all that God has intended for us as couples, and we can easily take our marriages to a new level of fulfillment.

Once we understand God's purpose for the marriage and God's principles for the marriage, our eyes are opened, and we wonder why we didn't see these simple truths long ago. There is a reason. We are creatures of this world, and we are conditioned by our world to think and act and react in certain ways. But the ways of the world are not helpful, as witnessed by the growing trend toward divorce, illegitimacy and cohabitation.

It is time to break loose from the mold, break loose from the hindrances, break loose from the traditions and wrong concepts that keep us from making progress and, thus, begin taking marriage to a higher level of fulfillment.

Neil Rhodes
Denver, Colorado

NOLINE'S PERSPECTIVE

I would like to express my thanks to our Lord and Savior for the great thing He has done in our marriage. To Him be all the glory.

I must also thank Neil, my loving husband, for being faithful to the challenge and call that God has placed on his life to follow God's plan for marriage and to teach others to do the same. Neil, I love you with all my heart.

It is wonderful to see what God can do when we are willing to take His Word to heart and apply it to our daily lives. When Neil and I first married, we had great ideals of what our relationship should be like. But we were both selfish and each expected the other to make whatever changes were necessary to make our dream into a reality.

Neither of us had any understanding of what God meant when He said that He would make us "one flesh." Since He promised it, we expected it to happen – automatically and without any effort on our part. What a shock it was for us when we woke up

9

one day to realize that not only didn't we have the ideal relationship we had expected to develop together, we didn't even love each other any longer and were actually considering divorce as the best option for our future happiness. Not a moment too late we turned to the One who has practical answers for our lives – Jesus, and He turned our lives around and put our marriage back together.

Because of our decision to turn to God and to learn His will for marriage, we are enjoying happiness and fulfillment in our relationship. Our marriage has been restored physically, emotionally and spiritually. Neil has learned to be more Christlike and not to Lord it over me. I have the freedom to express myself – as a woman, as a wife and as a child of God. And for that I am thankful.

It is our joy now to work with hundreds of other couples who have suffered as we did. To each of you I say, God is no respecter of persons and what He has done for us, He can also do for you. If you are willing to learn His principles and apply them, you can also *"Take Your Marriage to a Higher Level of Fulfillment."*

I pray that this book will be a blessing to you and will help you to start *"Breaking Loose"* from your old patterns of thinking, that your heart may be changed toward each other and your first love be restored.

Noline Rhodes

CHAPTER ONE

FORGETTING THE OLD AND LEARNING THE NEW

Therefore, get rid of all moral filth and the evil that is so prevalent and accept the word that is planted in you, which can save you. Do not merely listen to the word, and so deceive yourselves. Do what it says. Anyone who listens to the word but does not do what it says is like a man who looks at his face in the mirror and, after looking at himself, goes away and immediately forgets what he looks like. But the man who looks intently into the perfect law that brings freedom, and continues to do this, not forgetting what he has heard, but doing it — he will be blest in what he does.   James 1:21-25

I remember the day when I was five years old and the Queen Mother came to our town. We were living in Northern Rhodesia at the time, and my parents had dressed us all up in our Sunday best for the occasion. I held a small Union Jack in my hands and waved it back and forth as the royal cavalcade went by. What a memorable day it was!

I was too young at the time to understand what an impact Britain had made on its colonies around the world, but as I grew I came to realize that the British influence was unmistakable and far-reaching. I have since witnessed this truth over and over again around the world, in both present and former British domains.

In the sixteenth century, under the leadership of Queen Elizabeth I, England had risen from a small island kingdom with no overseas possessions to defeat the "invincible" Spanish Armada and to take over many of the Spanish and Portuguese trade routes and, thus, to begin building a worldwide empire. Parts of that empire were taken by conquest, while other parts were added through discovery and settlement. Before that exciting period of expansion ended, Great Britain ruled lands on every continent and islands in every ocean. It was a common and accepted saying that the sun never set on Britain's dominions.

Those of us living in the African colonies were thousands of miles from the British Isles, yet the traditions of that small place affected our lives in so many ways. Just like children in the Caribbean and South America who grew up in British lands, we all wore school uniforms and played cricket, soccer, and rugby. The examinations we took in high school were all graded in England and mailed back to us, wherever we happened to be, so that we could all maintain uniformity in our academic achievements.

In many other similar ways, the roots of our heritage went very deep. And now, many years after the British Empire dissolved into dozens of independent and sovereign countries, the people in most of those former British colonies still drive on the left side of the road, and still eat

Forgetting the Old and Learning the New

in the traditional British way, with knife and fork (with the fork held in the left hand, upside down — requiring a delicate balancing act to keep the peas on the back of its curve). Most of those countries have copied the British form of parliamentarian government as well.

There was one great advantage in being raised in this way. When we went to visit the Motherland, we always felt right at home. The disadvantage for me came when as an adult, with my patterns in life well set, I was suddenly thrust into a new and very strange environment.

In 1982, my wife and I and our three small children immigrated to the United States to pastor a church in South Dakota. We suddenly felt that we had been caught up in a time warp and thrust thirty years into the future. Some aspects of the change were absolutely delightful. We had never seen grocery stores filled with so many food items, and they were open twenty-four hours a day. Fast food chains were something totally new and pleasing to us, as all of our meals in Africa had been home-cooked.

But there was a definite down side to the experience, an inescapable culture shock. No matter how much we had read or studied about the United States, nothing could have prepared us for the far different life here. You had to experience it to believe it.

We are convinced that what helped us to adapt to American life was our willingness to reserve judgment until we better understood a particular custom, to keep an open mind about everything and everyone. We didn't come here with a "know-it-all attitude." Thank God! And the more we learned about our new country, and the more we practiced living what we were taught, the faster we were able to adapt to our new surroundings.

For instance, we had never seen snow before, and that proved to be a serious matter because South Dakota, after all, was "snow country." Some friends told us that when it began to snow we should get out and start shoveling our driveway. If we didn't get the snow off before it built up, they said, it would be there all winter, and we wouldn't be able to get in the driveway.

We had never heard of such a thing, but soon we had our first major snowstorm of the year, which produced fully two feet of accumulation. We decided that they knew what they were talking about, so we were the first ones out that day shoveling the snow. The local television station happened to have a mobile unit in the neighborhood, and they taped us "Africans" out shoveling snow.

What if we hadn't been willing to heed that good advice? What if we had refused to have a teachable spirit? I'm afraid we would have suffered a lot in adjusting to our new surroundings.

We had to learn to drive on the right side of the road and to use automobiles whose transmissions automatically shifted from one gear to the next. What a different life for us!

It actually took us a couple of years before we felt fully adjusted to the American lifestyle, one which we have come to love and appreciate very much. But if we had come to this country with our minds made up, sure that we knew what was right, that we were not about to change from the customs with which we grew up, and that we would not obey laws that were foreign to us, we surely would never have been able to adapt to a new cultural environment. And we would have been miserable as a result.

Imagine insisting on driving on the left side of the road here in the United States! Not only would this have endangered our lives and the lives of others, but it is against the law, and we might have been arrested for doing it. We simply had to make the change or else lose the right to drive on the American highways. In order to embrace the full potential of our lives as Americans, we first had to break loose from our old mindset. That may sound easy, but it was anything but easy.

We have known many other families who made the move from various British colonies to the United States, and it was apparent that they were not willing to make the necessary adjustments in order to enjoy life here. They immigrated in body, but not in mind or spirit. We call these people "the when-we's" because in nearly every conversation they can be heard to say, "When we were in Africa, life was much better," or "When we were in Africa, we had many more friends," "When we were in Africa, the food was much better," and "When we were in Africa, we always had lots of sunshine."

As good as life is in the United States, it is a miserable life for people like them. They want to keep living here because they enjoy the prosperity, the conveniences, and the opportunities American life provides, but in their minds, they are still living past memories. They are no different than the Israelites who, on their way to the promised land, began to hunger for the leeks and garlics of Egypt. They should have been so glad to be free of

Egypt that they would never again complain, but they, instead, refused to adjust to life on the way to the land of milk and honey.

A very similar thing happens when we make a decision to leave the kingdom of darkness and to become part of God's Kingdom of Light. We have grown up under the laws of this world, and when we get saved it seems as though we have immigrated spiritually, but perhaps not mentally and physically. Many of us try desperately to live out the new life of the Kingdom of God through the mindset of our old natures. This can only make us miserable Christians.

Paul wrote to the Ephesians:

> *You were taught, with regard to your former way of life, to put off your old self, which is being corrupted by its deceitful desires; to be made new in the attitude of your minds; and to put on the new self, created to be like God in true righteousness and holiness.* Ephesians 4:22-24

A person who refused to make the change from driving on the left side of the road (as I legally did for many years in Africa) to the right side of the road (as is required in this country) would place himself and others in imminent danger. So it is in the Christian life. We simply cannot fail to make the necessary changes, from the kingdom of this world to God's Kingdom. And if we do fail to change, we can never fully experience all that God has prepared for us through Christ.

Just as Africa and America have very different cultures, the differences in the cultures of the two spiritual kingdoms are immense. Could this be the reason that many Christians seem to have just enough Christianity to make them miserable? We should be the happiest people on the face of the earth, for we have much to celebrate. Yet going to church, reading the Bible, and praying are still a chore for many who call themselves Christians. Surely they hover between two worlds, unwilling to leave the old in order to fully appropriate the benefits of the new. If we expect to enjoy Christianity at its fullest, we must make a complete commitment to God's Kingdom, willingly and gladly leave behind the traditions of the past, and get into the Kingdom — body, soul and spirit!

When Christ is only an addition to an already busy lifestyle, and where He is given a portion of a life but not all of it, we must recognize that as pseudo-Christianity. When this is the case, Jesus is not really Lord of our lives. He expects us to be converted totally if we want to live in His kingdom, to place ourselves squarely under His laws, and to allow Him to govern us, as He wills. Disappointment and discouragement occur when we desire the advantages and blessings of living in God's Kingdom, but we also want to retain the right to make our own rules concerning how we will live out our "Christian experience."

What does all this have to do with marriage? First, if we live our married lives according to the customs and teachings of the world, we are headed for disaster. But there is a second way in which these truths affect us: When two people decide to be joined together in holy matrimony, they are making a radical decision. They are each giving up the life they have lived as singles and are entering into a totally new life, a life together, as partners in marriage. They are exchanging their two single lives for one new life, which they will share. This exchange should be welcomed by both partners as they determine to learn to live a new lifestyle — in just the same way we learned to live a new lifestyle in our adopted country. But because many married people have not learned this lesson, they find themselves to be absolutely miserable. They want to continue to live as single people, while enjoying the benefits of married life. And it doesn't work.

Too many married people have not yet realized that their lives must change. No one has taught them this truth, and no one has called them into account when they fall short of its requirements. If marriage is to succeed, the two partners in marriage cannot go on living as two single people. The mentality of singleness must die, and a totally new and different mentality must be allowed to take its place.

My wife and I found that we could not live in Africa and America at the same time. It was one or the other. If we chose to be Americans and to enjoy all the benefits that choice entailed, it meant that we had to leave Africa and "Africanness" — if I could be allowed to coin a word to express my thoughts. Couples who want to live by the world's standards and still expect to receive God's blessings on their marriage will be disappointed. And couples who expect to enjoy the pleasures of married life while still retaining the freedoms of singleness will be disappointed as well.

Forgetting the Old and Learning the New

What would people think of me if I insisted that I am not answerable to the laws of America because I grew up somewhere else and find these laws to be foreign? What would people think of me if I tried to insist that everyone in America drive on the left, just because that's the way I happened to learn it, and I feel more comfortable with it that way? No, I am the one who must adjust, not the other way around, if I expect to continue enjoying the benefits of American life.

It is impossible to live in the world, with all its pleasures, and still expect to be recognized as a Christian and to call Heaven your home. Living such a life is called "lukewarmness," or "carnality." The Bible answered it, when it said:

> *If anyone loves the world, the love of the Father is*
> *not in him.*   1 John 2:15

It is impossible to be blessed as long as you insist on living for the world and for Christ at the same time. It is nothing but halfhearted Christianity, and if you try to do the same thing with your marriage relationship, you will have a halfhearted marriage.

The only reason I feel free to say many of these things is that I experienced them first hand. After twelve years of married life, Noline and I asked the Lord one day how we were doing in our relationship. While we were still praying, He answered us by giving us a word picture of a baby in diapers and telling us that our marriage needed to grow up. Shocked, we discovered that we had missed

19

so much in our lives, because we were living like married singles, after all those years.

I had pursued my own goals in life, and Noline had pursued hers. Mine had been ministry-oriented, so I felt justified in pursuing them as an individual, rather than as a couple. I was serving God, and I was serving Him with all my heart. Noline's goals, on the other hand, had been more family oriented. There was certainly nothing wrong with that, and she had felt perfectly justified in pursuing those goals, as an individual rather than doing it as a couple. It was her family, and, for her, family always came first. We were two single people trying to make a marriage work. No wonder we failed and had to start all over!

Our insistence on living individual lives created enormous conflicts that never seemed to find resolution, and it made us both miserable. We were traveling in two different directions at the same time.

On top of all this, I fell into adultery and sinned against my God and against my wife. It happened not just once, but twice. These foolish acts created heartache and bitterness and brought the fiber of our relationship to the breaking point. We remained together only for the sake of our children.

It was not until we recognized the immaturity of our relationship and began to apply the laws of God's Word to our individual lives and to the marriage that we began to break loose from the past and to find the rewards we had always looked for in our union. Once we learned the biblical principles of marriage and began to apply them to our own daily lives, we immediately began to see a difference.

As a couple, we began to make the transition from the life of two singles to the life of two joined by God as one — in purpose and in expression. The single attitude began to die in each of us, and we were miraculously yoked together in a new life of unity. What a miracle!

James wrote to the churches of the first century that if they expected to be blessed in this life they must learn to live according to God's laws. He encouraged them to *"get rid"* of the old life and to *"accept"* the new life God was offering them. They needed to break loose. It was not enough, he taught them, to simply hear or to know the Word of God. They needed to obey it.

Talk like this makes many people nervous. When they hear about laws and rules and principles, they feel that someone is trying to take away their freedom. But just the opposite is true. The Word of God is a law that *"brings freedom."* The law that tells me to drive on the right side of the road in America is not something that has put me in bondage, and I do not resent it. It has loosed me to be free to enjoy the American highways. It seemed strange at first, and it took me a while to adjust to my new surroundings, but it was all for my benefit, for my good. Why should I rail against that?

In the very same way, the laws of the Kingdom of God are not laws that restrict us or rob us of God's best. These laws bring us true freedom, and God has every right to urge us to obey them. Indeed, He would be remiss not to do so. Otherwise, James showed us, we are like the man who looked in the mirror and then quickly forgot what he looked like. Without God's principles, influence and guidance, we have no way of knowing or understanding what we are all about and what our true potential is.

Marriage, like everything else in life, needs guidelines, and God has provided those guidelines. If we are willing to follow His outline for marriage, the result will be a new freedom to become everything God has called us to be as husband and wife, a breaking loose to take our marriage to a higher level of fulfillment than we have ever imagined possible.

Chapter Two

Preparing For Transition

As Jesus was coming up out of the water, he saw heaven being torn open and the Spirit descending on him like a dove. And a voice came from heaven: "You are my Son, whom I love; with you I am well pleased." At once the Spirit sent him out into the desert, and he was in the desert forty days, being tempted by Satan. He was with the wild animals, and angels attended him.   Mark 1:10-13

Before Jesus began His public ministry, He was first baptized in the River Jordan. Baptism signifies a death to the old life and a resurrection into the new. It would seem that Jesus didn't need that, for He was the sinless Son of God. Yet He said that He had done it *"to fulfill all righteousness."* He was about to enter into a new and very different stage of His life — a very different life, if you will. He would no longer be the Jesus who had grown up in the house of Joseph and Mary. His life would now be wholly committed to doing the will of His heavenly Father. And if He was to be successful in what He was called to do, if He was to fulfill His destiny as *"the Lamb of God slain from the foundation of the world,"* He must now make a great transition. He would no longer be *"the carpenter's son."* He would now be *"the Son of God."* The old must be laid down and the new embraced, so that the man, Jesus of Nazareth, could become the Savior of the world.

There were four interesting steps that Jesus made in His transition into public ministry. First, Jesus received a revelation. Secondly, Jesus was anointed. Thirdly, Jesus was identified or confirmed. And, finally, Jesus set Himself apart in a desert place and meditated on the Word of God for an extended period of time in preparation for His work. Let us briefly examine these four steps, since we also want to make a transition ourselves, into a new level of fulfillment in our married lives.

As Jesus was coming out of the water of the Jordan, He saw Heaven opened. In other words, He received a revelation. He saw the angels attending the throne of God and the magnificent glory of the presence of the Father. Once He had seen that glory and it was firmly imbedded in His heart and mind, there would be no question of whether or not the road to the cross was worth the price He must pay. Jesus had seen into the future and knew what the outcome would be — if He was willing to fulfill the will of the Father. Such a revelation would certainly make anything on earth seem small and unimportant by comparison.

The second thing that happened to Jesus, as He was dedicating Himself to a new life of ministry, was that the Spirit descended upon Him in the form of a dove. This was the Father's provision of anointing which Jesus would need for His public ministry. He had come to earth as a man and would need the power of the Holy Spirit working in and through Him to complete all that the Father now required of Him. Every miracle that was performed by Jesus in the days ahead and all the wisdom and knowledge that He would impart to those who sought Him, were a direct result of the power of the Holy Spirit that came upon His life that day. Without the intervention of the Holy Spirit in our lives, we are nothing, and we can do nothing of spiritual value.

The third thing that happened to Jesus, as He made the transition from private citizen to servant of all mankind, was that a voice came from Heaven, confirming that He was indeed the Son of God and that the Father was *"well pleased"* with Him. We could call this identification, and nothing could be more wonderful than identification from God Himself. Once He had received this divine identification, Jesus no longer needed the approval or the validation of men, and he had no need to submit himself or subject himself to the wisdom of men. He knew where He had come from, where He was going, and exactly what He was called to do here on earth. Man's wisdom could add nothing to that knowledge.

Once Jesus had received the revelation, and the anointing, and the identification of the Father, He separated Himself for the next forty days in fasting and prayer in a desert place. Very little is written in Scripture about this place or what transpired there, but we can imagine that Jesus spent a great deal of time during those forty days contemplating what He had seen and felt and experienced at the Jordan.

To see the heavens opened, to receive the power of God, and to have clarified in your mind and heart your purpose in life is something very wonderful, to which we should all aspire. Surely Jesus pondered all this in the light of the totality of the Scriptures during the weeks of His seclusion. For forty days, He waited upon God until He was ready to go forth and face His assigned task.

There are so many lessons to be learned here. We are certainly no better than Jesus, and if we want to make the transition from the thinking of the world to the principles of God's Kingdom, and if we expect to make the difficult transition from single mentality to a state of marital bliss, it is important for us to follow the same four steps.

First, we need a revelation of what marriage really is. This God-ordained relationship is based on a covenant and not on a contract. Marriage is far more than a piece of paper issued by some governmental agency. It is a commitment to a lifelong relationship and has God as its most important witness. Whether the two parties are standing before a justice of the peace, before a pastor in a church, or before a tribal leader in a remote place of the earth, that doesn't change the meaning and importance of the vows they make to each other. Marriage is a sacred pact, instituted by God Himself, and He expects us to keep our part of the bargain.

As Christians, we have the privilege of sharing every part of our lives with God, but the God of the Universe holds every man responsible for the sacred vows he makes, believer and unbeliever alike. Therefore, each of us must get a revelation of what marriage really is. The Scriptures declare:

> *Where there is no revelation, the people cast off restraint;*   Proverbs 29:18

26

Preparing For Transition

Without a revelation, you can never expect to make the complete transition to what the Bible expects for married couples. No wonder so many people are divorcing! They have no revelation. They have no knowledge of what God expects of them. They signed a contract, but it was no more than a piece of paper to them. If their spouse is not bringing them happiness, they feel that they have the "right" to break the marriage vows and to free themselves from the relationship.

Many married people still expect to have the freedom to come and go that they enjoyed when they were still single, and that will never change — unless and until they get a revelation of what marriage was intended to be. In marriage, the good of the relationship takes precedence over the whims of the individual, and not many understand that fact. We are no longer two independent individuals; we are now one flesh.

Many of the difficulties Noline and I experienced in the early years of our life together could have been avoided if we had known what we know now, that we must die to self in order to live in full freedom and happiness together.

Jesus had a revelation, and we need a revelation, if we are to succeed as a couple.

Jesus was anointed by the Spirit. In this regard, we believers have a distinct advantage in married life. The Spirit of God can lead us and can teach us His ways. Noline and I, however, often chose to disregard the promptings of the Holy Spirit and to disobey His leadings. Instead of drawing on His strength in times of difficulty in our relationship, we withdrew into ourselves and brooded over our problems.

The power which the Holy Spirit brings into the life of the believer is crucial for making the transition from singleness to life together as *"one flesh."* Death to self is not an easy thing, and the only way we can achieve it is to replace that death with life, the life of the Spirit of God. For all those who are willing, the Holy Spirit will give the power to rise up above all human weakness and frailty and to do what God requires of us. But, just as we can do nothing else useful and holy without His power, the miracle of the union of two distinct and very different individuals into *"one flesh"* is impossible without His intervention. Only God can take two individual human beings, with all their differences (and with all their corresponding strengths and weaknesses), and forge them into one powerful and fruitful unit called matrimony. It is foolish, therefore, to rely on the wisdom of men in this regard.

No wonder so many are divorcing! Only God, the Creator of marriage, has the wisdom to guide us in these difficult decisions. We must be filled daily with His Spirit and learn to depend on Him more and more. If Jesus needed the power of the Holy Spirit to do the work assigned to Him, how much more we need Him today!

Jesus received His identification from the Father, and so must we. Many people come from dysfunctional homes where parents have not understood the purpose and function of marriage, and where everyone involved got hurt, especially the children. If we rely on our background or our family tradition to give us our sole identification, we will surely err seriously. The lack of proper role models is one of the world's most common laments. Because the people of this present generation have abused their marriage vows and done what is convenient, what can we expect of the next generation? And the next? A vicious and disastrous cycle has developed.

Our identity must not come only from our natural parents or from the so-called "specialists" in the field of marriage, but from God Himself. If not, we have no hope of success.

When we were first married, we both noticed that Noline had difficulty trusting God to hear and answer prayer. Then the Holy Spirit began to minister to her about her relationship to her father. He was a workaholic who didn't seem to have time for his children, let alone give them the love and attention they so desperately needed to develop properly. Noline remembers an incident that demonstrates his attitude:

All the children were in the living room one day playing, and making an awful racket. The noise finally disturbed Noline's mother, and she called out to her husband, "Trevor, speak to the children." The amazing thing was that Trevor had been sitting right there reading the newspaper, and had been oblivious to it all. He very calmly lowered the paper now and said, "Children, I'm speaking to you." He looked up at his wife and asked, "Are you happy, Dear?" Then he again raised his newspaper to eye level and went on reading as before. To Trevor, his children seemed to be just fixtures in the house, nothing more.

Deep down, Noline came away from this early experience with her father's indifference thinking that God must be much too busy with the important affairs of the world to be bothered with her. It took her time to overcome her negative mindset and to trust God, that He was different, and that He was always available to listen to those who call upon Him and to help them in their time of need. Sadly, the great majority of the children of this world identify God with their father. And that can be a tragedy, especially if they were abusive and not kind and loving. More than ever before, we need to find our identification in Christ.

Husbands and wives must first be children of the Living God, with His character planted in them through His Word, and with His destiny in their hearts. Then, when they come together in marriage, they will see each other first in this light, and then secondly as mates.

Arriving at this goal is not automatic, in any sense of the word. When we have the revelation of what our potential is in God, when His Spirit has anointed us, and when we have received our identification direct from Heaven, there is still a lot of meditating required, if we are to understand the hows and whys and wherefores of God. Unless we are willing to meditate on the scriptures that relate to the marriage covenant and to the one-flesh relationship and have them firmly fixed in our hearts and minds, we will never be able to live them. Because we are living in the midst of a generation accustomed to instant gratification, and which is largely unwilling to accept blame for its failures, being willing to learn, to accept, and to obey God's priorities is our only hope of success.

Meditating on the Scriptures helps us to count the cost and decide if we are willing to commit to the life He lays

Preparing For Transition

out for us. Once that decision is made, His Spirit will empower us to keep those commitments. Then, as life's storms arise, the Word of God guides us step by step into facing and resolving every difficult situation. But unless we are willing to take the time to ponder these truths and to get them into our hearts, they can do us no good.

The writer of Hebrews quoted the Psalmist, when he said:

> *Today, if you hear his voice, do not harden your hearts.*   Hebrews 4:7

Noline and I, having been through the thirteen-week course of Marriage Ministries International, spent more than two years of study in the Word, with much time spent in Christian libraries, before we settled into the full revelation of what God had for marriage. Little by little, God's truth began to seep through our old patterns of thinking and light dawned in our hearts. Today we are totally committed to building our *"one-flesh"* relationship. And we believe that we will leave a lasting legacy for our children, something that we consider far more important than a financial inheritance. They will be the immediate benefactors of our relationship, and their own marriages and those of their children will be enriched by our example.

Make preparations for your transition, from the old to the new, from the single to the married, from the world's ways to God's ways. It is time to break loose from the traditions that are robbing you of God's best for your life, and to move on into a much higher level of fulfillment in your marriage.

CHAPTER THREE

UNDERSTANDING THE CONCEPT OF COVENANT

So God created man in his own image, in the image of God he created him; male and female he created them. God blessed them and said to them, "Be fruitful and increase in number; fill the earth and subdue it. Rule over the fish of the sea and the birds of the air and over every living creature that moves on the ground." Genesis 1:27-28

Od intended marriage to be fruitful and blessed, not just with children, as many commonly interpret this passage, but with His favor. In order for God to bless marriage, however, as He intended from the beginning, the man and the woman must be willing to keep their part of the marriage covenant. So each of us needs to have a better understanding of just what is meant by covenant.

Many people are unwilling even to explore the meaning of covenant because they see it as too restrictive, when, in reality, it is just the opposite. Covenant commitment is freeing and fulfilling. It frees us from the expectations of the world, and it frees God to bless us as He desires. When both spouses understand the power of covenant, they can be free to be themselves without having to constantly perform for acceptance. The marriage covenant also gives us purpose and destiny as a couple, and that is exciting.

We can see God's intention in the Garden of Eden when, under the Adamic Covenant, He gave Adam and Eve the privilege to live a life free from concern. He gave them unlimited access to the tree of life. And He gave them access to His presence. He came to walk with them in the Garden *"in the cool of the day."* They were free to enjoy everything that they found in the Garden and free to partake of any of the fruits of the Garden, except one. There is no way anyone could describe this life as restrictive. It was anything but restrictive.

The fact that all that was lost when Adam and Eve fell should not restrict us in reaching our full potential, because it was restored to us through Christ. In fact, the word *salvation* (*sozo*, in the original Greek) means "healing, preservation, keeping and deliverance." This is not restrictive at all. This is freedom.

When people look at marriage and its covenant, and realize that worldly pleasures are no longer appropriate when we come to Christ, they take that in a negative and restrictive way. The fact is that when God requires us to lay down the lesser, He gives us the greater in its place, and we lose nothing. He takes our sentence of death and gives us His promise of life.

Some worry about being able to give up a lifestyle they have lived for many years, and that is understandable. We can't do that in our own strength, but we can do it in Christ's strength. This is why Jesus said:

Understanding the Concept of Covenant

*I tell you the truth, anyone who will not receive the
kingdom of God like a little child will never enter it.*
Mark 10:15

Children do not have a lot to unlearn, so they make the
transition to new things with great ease. We must be the
same, for we must not lose the benefits of the marriage
covenant through ignorance or stubbornness.

Those of us who grew up in the Western culture, usually think of marriage as a contract between two people.
But, as we have said, it is much more than that. God
never intended for the marriage covenant to be limited in
liability, which is exactly what a contract offers. He intended it to be a lifelong covenant, with unlimited
liability.

When we take our wedding vows, we say to each other
"till death us do part." The vows are based on the Bible and
on God's idea of what a marriage agreement should be.
Civil ceremonies are often worded differently, but even
there, a strong godly influence is seen. For God is the author of marriage, and He knows what He intended
marriage to be.

Those who are born-again have a great advantage in
marriage. We have access to the love, power, forgiveness
and strength of God, to sustain our relationship through
every storm of life. A contract cannot offer such benefits.
Marriage without God is indeed something very different.

The worst aspect of viewing marriage as a mere legal
contract is that it can be broken. There are always loop-
hole clauses in contracts to cover one when business

partners and associates fail to see eye to eye and come to a parting of the ways. The agreement can be broken. Contracts are man-made, so they depend on the strength and ingenuity of the parties involved. Covenant, however, is God-made, so it relies on His strength and wisdom, a much safer bet.

COVENANT AND THE WIFE

Who has left the partner of her youth and ignored the covenant she made before God.

Proverbs 2:17

Every woman is responsible before God for the covenant she made when she entered into marriage. That responsibility is not dependent on where the marriage occurred, or when, or under what circumstance. God was the silent witness to that marriage covenant into which she entered, and He holds her responsible to be faithful. The fact that her husband may fail in some way does not annul the covenant, so the wife has no right to break it or walk away from it.

Too many people have viewed their marriage as a contract and, therefore, believed that the failure of their spouse granted them freedom to nullify the agreement. But our marriage covenant is a lifelong commitment, and we are liable for our part of covenant — as long as we live.

Paul wrote to the Galatians:

Brothers, let me take an example from everyday life. Just as no one can set aside or add to a human cov-

Understanding the Concept of Covenant

enant that has been duly established, so it is in this case.   Galatians 3:15

On our wedding day, Noline came down the aisle dressed in her beautiful white wedding dress, her father at her side. As she came toward me, I stepped out into the aisle to meet her and take her to the altar, and there she spoke forth the words of her vows before God, before me, and before the witnesses present. We had rehearsed the format of our ceremony before the actual day arrived and knew exactly what we were going to say. We had agreed together that what we were saying was exactly what we wanted to say. There were no surprises.

Until the actual pronouncement of our union by the minister, we had time to change our minds, to change the wording of the vows we intended to take, or to choose not to repeat the vows at all. But we didn't do that. We *wanted* to make those vows. We *wanted* to live together in harmony and to bring each other happiness. So, at the altar of the church, before the minister, before God, and before the other witnesses present, we made our vows to each other.

It was January 13, 1973, and from that day on, Noline has been responsible before God to be faithful to the covenant she made with me and with Him at that altar. That fact didn't change when, after only a few years of marriage, I violated my vows and committed adultery against her. My breaking the vows, however, did not release her from her commitment. A spouse's failure is no reason for you to fail, too!

COVENANT AND THE HUSBAND

In the same way, the husband is responsible before God for the covenant he makes:

> *Because you [the husband] have broken faith with her, though she is your partner, the wife of your marriage covenant.* Malachi 2:14

The man who has made a vow before God is responsible to carry out that vow and be faithful to it. He cannot use either his wife's failure or his own as an excuse to break the vow he made. His vow to his wife is lifelong and irreversible. If his wife has failed to keep her covenant with him, it is still no excuse and does not give the husband the right to annul a covenant that he made before God.

The day I stood before the Lord at the altar, no one was holding a gun to my head. No one was forcing me to make those vows to my wife. I *wanted* to do it, and I did it freely and voluntarily, even gladly. Indeed, it was a day of great joy for both of us. Therefore, just because circumstances have changed in the meantime does not give me the right to back out of the agreement I made on January 13, 1973. I am just as responsible today as I was then, for the words I spoke before the altar, when I vowed my faithfulness to my wife *"till death us do part."*

THE ORIGINS OF THE MARRIAGE COVENANT

If marriage had been ordained by men, we might have

reason to wonder if it could succeed. It wasn't. Marriage was established by God because He foresaw something wonderful would come of it. By joining a man and a woman to be one flesh, He could make one effective and powerful unit. God created the man, and God created the woman, but He foresaw that neither one of them would accomplish the fullness of their potential, unless He made them a team.

When God brought the first woman to Adam, and he saw her for the first time, he was delighted and said, *"This is now bone of my bone and flesh of my flesh"* (Genesis 2:23).

Since Genesis is the book of beginnings and establishes the laws governing man and his relationship, the standard established in Genesis was an eternal one and can be traced all the way through the rest of the Bible. It was, therefore, intended by God to be carried out by men and women of all generations to come throughout all the days of their lives.

God decided that one man and one woman should be joined to form a family unit. This is His standard, and He allowed it to be documented and forever recorded in His written Word. God's plan for marriage is, therefore, firmly established.

When we break our marriage covenant, we are not just hurting the other person involved, we are going against the clear teaching of God's Word and what we are doing can only be classified as "wrong" and "sin." If God's standard seems inconvenient to men, that doesn't change it. We have no right to change it, for any reason.

In recent years, Christians have chosen to follow the

pattern of worldly counselors, rather than obey God's principles for marriage. This has resulted in a rash of divorces in the church. Instead of setting a pattern for others to follow, as God intended, we have chosen to accept the easy way out. This is sad.

Instead of consistently proving God's perfect will for marriage, Christians have searched for ways to justify divorce, and this has set loose a runaway freight train that is wreaking havoc on the Body of Christ. This unbridled force surges through the church, leaving in its wake ruined homes, single parents, and a generation of children to be raised under difficult circumstances. This leaves the generation to come with no clear picture of what God intended a marriage covenant to be. May God help us in this hour!

Long ago, Noline and I made the decision to remove the word "divorce" from our vocabulary. We know that the devil looks for any open door that he can find to harm our relationship, so we refuse to give him that opening. He knows that if a person considers divorce for any reason, he can push them toward that door, until they finally decide to leave their spouses. Since this is not what God wants, we have taken a stand against it, personally and publicly.

Very early in our own marriage we were both guilty of trying to use fear tactics with each other. I would say, "If you ever cheat on me, I'm out of here." Noline would say, "If you ever hit me, you'll never see me again." We used that threat of divorce or separation, all the while, hoping that this would secure our relationship. But fear is not an effective tool. The only thing fear delivers is *"torment."* It cannot guarantee faithfulness in the marriage.

After I had fallen into an adulterous relationship, No-line was advised that she should divorce me, and that seemed like good advice at the time. She was so wounded emotionally that anger and pride filled her heart, and divorce would be a way of avenging the wrong done to her. The fact that friends encouraged her to do it seemed to make it easier to contemplate. Her decision to stay with me was probably only due to the fact that I had repented of my error and desperately wanted to stay in the relationship, and perhaps, because deep down inside, she knew what God had to say on the subject. Today, we are thankful that she made the right choice, even though we had limited understanding of the teachings of Scripture concerning marriage as covenant.

Even when there is no repentance on the part of the wayward spouse and he or she does not seem to want the marriage to work, covenant commitment is still the correct approach for the wronged spouse. It will unlock God's power to touch the heart of the spouse in sin. Covenant commitment says, *"Stand ... and see the salvation of the Lord."*

THE EXCEPTION CLAUSE

Christians have discovered what many are calling "the exception clause," and they seem to be very happy about that discovery. It gives them an excuse to break their marriage vows. Now, when a Christian wants to break off the marital relationship, he or she calls up "the exception clause." The line goes like this: My spouse has been unfaithful to me. I am the "innocent party" in all of this. I deserve happiness myself, so I consider myself free to leave this relationship and to enter into another, if I care to do so.

Thus, over and over again, Christian men and women are forsaking their mates, and feeling justified in their actions, forgetting that they themselves made a vow before God on their wedding day that the relationship formed by those vows would last *"till death us do part."*

It doesn't seem to matter any longer that God has plainly set forth His will in the Holy Bible. We prefer to accept a worldly theology and to try to make it fit into Kingdom principles.

But what about that "exception clause"?

I have personally come to believe that Matthew 19:9, where so many Christians have found their so-called "exception clause," refers not to adultery after the wedding night, but to the betrothal period. It was to this Jewish law that Joseph referred when he learned that Mary was expecting a child before they had become sexually intimate. Because of the law, he had a right to set aside his commitment to her, if indeed she had betrayed him with another man. This was, in fact, Joseph's first consideration. He knew Mary to be a good woman and was determined not to put her through a public humiliation, so he had decided to put her away (divorce her) privately. It was only through the intervention of an angel, who spoke to him in a dream, that he knew Mary had not been unfaithful and that he should not forsake her.

Understanding the Concept of Covenant

The Law stated, in Deuteronomy 22, that if uncleanness was found in a man's betrothed wife prior to their marriage night , he could divorce her, and he could do it "without penalty." If no uncleanness was found in her, however, he was denied that option. The law was so strict that an unclean woman could even be publicly stoned for this offense.

A common practice, then, in Old Testament times, was to place a clean white sheet on the bed during the first night the couple was together. The blood that resulted, when the hymen of the virgin was broken, stained the sheets, and this became the parents' "proof of virginity," the evidence they would produce if any claim of impurity was made against their daughter in the future. Once this proof of virginity was produced, the husband had no case against his wife and could not discredit her, even if he wanted to.

Engagement today is both similar and dissimilar to that of Joseph's time. It is similar in that the two parties make a pledge to each other to prepare for their marriage. It is dissimilar in that it is not as binding as a legal marriage, and it was just that binding when Joseph and Mary were betrothed.

This, to my way of thinking, was the only setting in which the so-called "exception clause" applied. The Scriptures make it very clear that God's will for the believer is to stay in the marriage:

> *And I say unto you, Whosoever shall put away his*
> *wife, except it be for fornication, and shall marry*

another, committeth adultery: and whoso marrieth her which is put away doth commit adultery.

Matthew 19:9 (KJV)

Anyone who divorces his wife and marries another woman commits adultery against her. And if she divorces her husband and marries another man, she commits adultery.   Mark 10:11-12

By law a married woman is bound to her husband as long as he is alive, but if her husband dies, she is released from the law of marriage. So then, if she marries another man while her husband is still alive, she is called an adulteress. But if her husband dies, she is released from that law and is not an adulteress, even though she marries another man.

Romans 7:2-3

The Greek word translated here as *bound* literally means "chained." So a woman is "chained" to her husband *"while her husband is still alive."* This is a mutual bonding between a husband and wife. The two are "chained" together for life. Death, then, is the only release from the marriage bond. This is confirmed in Paul's letter to the Corinthians:

A woman is bound to her husband as long as he lives. But if her husband dies, she is free to marry anyone she wishes, but he must belong to the Lord.

1 Corinthians 7:39

Understanding the Concept of Covenant

This is covenant. God takes our covenants very seriously, and we should too. But, instead of looking for ways to obey God's commands, most people today are looking for ways to justify their mad rush for the exit.

THE MAD RUSH FOR THE EXIT

If you were eating in a restaurant, and a fire broke out in the far corner of the building, the first thing you would do is look for an exit. You would want to get out of that building just as fast as possible. That's logical.

With marriage, however, the exit sign is not God's way. He has a solution for every problem, and it is not to run away from the situation. Consider what might happen if you were in that same restaurant, and it was on fire, and you discovered that the doors were barred and chained so that you could not escape. What would you do in that case? I imagine we all might start thinking about how to put out the fire so that we would not perish in the blaze.

This picture is more in keeping with the way God views the marriage covenant. Instead of looking for the first available exit, we need to start looking for a way to resolve the problems we are facing. When God allows the fires of life to come to us, His intent is not that we be burned alive. Just as He was with Shadrach, Meshak and Abednego in the fiery furnace, He wants to be with every couple that refuses to flee the scene, but determines to stand their ground and fight the fires of adversity.

In the natural, most people don't even wait for the fire. As soon as they see a little smoke, they get out right way.

Let someone else handle the blaze. They are intent on saving themselves. Far too many Christians have adopted this easy and, seemingly, safe approach to facing life's trials. But where is our faith in God? Where is our sense of covenant responsibility?

A Second Escape Clause

There is another passage of Scripture that some Christians now use as an escape clause:

> *But if the unbeliever leaves, let him do so. A believing man or woman is not bound [literally, in bondage] in such circumstances; God has called us to live in peace.* 1 Corinthians 7:15

This passage has led many to believe that they are not bound to stay married to an unbeliever. This is not what the Apostle Paul was saying here. He was referring to the responsibility of a believer to bring his or her spouse to the faith. If the spouse resists, God is showing us, He has other ways of dealing with them. The next verse clarifies this point:

> *How do you know, wife, whether you will save your husband? Or, how do you know, husband, whether you will save your wife?* 1 Corinthians 7:16

Since marriage is a lifetime covenant, God is not releasing the saved spouse to divorce and remarry. He is releasing the saved spouse from thinking the only way to save his or her loved one is to keep that person in the home. God has other ways of dealing with them.

When the Philippian jailer was moved by the witness of God's favor upon Paul and Silas, a wonderful promise was given to him, a promise that we can all claim as our own, the promise that *"you will be saved"* and the additional promise *"and your household"* (Acts 16:31). When the Lord Jesus Christ is given authority over our households, He becomes Governor of the home, and He can and will bring each member of the family into His saving grace. It was because of this that Paul wrote that a believing spouse should not feel bound to try and keep the unbelieving spouse in the home, since that was not the only way that salvation could come to him. This portion of scripture, then, has nothing to do with releasing a person from his marriage vows so that he can be free to marry another. A marriage covenant never changes. It is timeless!

I know what everyone is saying these days: that we are living in the nineties, that times have changed, and that we need to catch up with the changing world. But God's standards never change. They are eternal, and they stand forever. There is no evolution with God's standards. Once He has established them in His Word, they remain unchanged for all eternity. He is never out-of-date!

Breaking your marriage vows is not an unforgivable sin, in any sense of the word. Human nature, when not submitted to the Lordship of Christ and to the principles of the Kingdom of God, makes decisions that are contrary to God's Word. And God has made provision for the fact that people sin against His perfect will, and "do their own thing," doing what feels good to them at the moment. That provision is called Calvary. The blood of Jesus Christ cleanses us from *all* sin.

GOD HATES DIVORCE

Those of us who love the Lord are not looking for justification for our sin. We want to please Him. So, when we realize that God hates divorce, and that remarriage is adulterous and goes against God's original plan for one man and one woman to be joined as "one flesh," we must make every effort to stop the runaway train that is destroying homes on every hand. This is not God's best for men and women anywhere. His will is clearly stated in the Bible:

> *Has not [the LORD] made them one? In flesh and spirit they are his. And why one? Because he was seeking godly offspring. So guard yourself in your spirit, and do not break faith with the wife of your youth. "I hate divorce," says the LORD God of Israel, "and I hate a man's covering himself with violence as well as with his garment," says the LORD Almighty. So guard yourself in your spirit, and do not break faith.* Malachi 2:15-16

God hates divorce. How could anything be more clear? Too many Christians have so saturated their minds with the compromise of Hollywood, where marriage is no longer held sacred, that they have accepted divorce and remarriage as a normal part of life. As a result, the

Understanding the Concept of Covenant

Body of Christ has become weakened in its stand on the vows made at the altar of God. He said:

> *If you make a vow to the Lord your God, do not be slow to pay it, for the Lord your God will certainly demand it of you and you will be guilty of sin. But if you refrain from making a vow, you will not be guilty. Whatever your lips utter you must be sure to do, because you made your vow freely to the Lord your God with your own mouth.*
>
> Deuteronomy 23:21-23

This doesn't mean that those who are divorced and remarried are condemned, and it isn't our desire to convey such condemnation in this writing. But if we are ever to turn around the present trend to hold the marriage commitment lightly, we must be willing to recognize that divorce and remarriage is not God's best, and that when we have disobeyed God's will for each of us, in any way, we should repent and recognize our wrongdoing.

If you have erred in this sense, I urge you first to repent, then to know that you are forgiven, then to receive that forgiveness and rejoice in it, and then to go forward with your life. If you refuse to recognize that you have sinned, you hinder God's blessing in your own life.

If you have set aside your marriage vows, if you have blamed your spouse for failure and used that failure as a reason to sin yourself, it is incumbent upon you to ask God's forgiveness, recognizing your own failure. He will forgive:

Breaking Loose

My dear children, I write this to you so that you will not sin. But if anybody does sin, we have one who speaks to the Father in our defense — Jesus Christ, the Righteous One.   1 John 2:1

If you have sinned against a former relationship and entered into a new one, repent of your sin so that your present relationship can be established on a firm foundation. Self-justification will never fix things. Only the blood of Jesus can cover our sins and provide us with a new beginning.

And, just as divorce is not the unpardonable sin, re-marriage is also not an unforgivable sin. Just as there is forgiveness for any other sin, there is forgiveness for this adulterous act as well. Just as there is a new beginning awaiting any man or woman who repents of sin, there is a new beginning awaiting any who have trangressed God's laws for marriage and are willing to recognize it and to start anew. You need not repeat the mistakes of the past.

This is not to say that we can go on living as we please and expect God to go on forgiving us. Sin always has dire consequences, and those who insist on continuing in sin put their relationship with the Lord in jeopardy.

Accepting the marriage covenant as God designed it will enable you to break loose from the limitations of the past and to take your marriage to a higher level of fulfillment. Why wait any longer?

CHAPTER FOUR

UNDERSTANDING THE ONE-FLESH RELATIONSHIP

For this reason a man will leave his father and mother and be united to his wife, and they will become one flesh.   Genesis 2:24

Therefore, what God has joined together, let not man separate.   Matthew 19:6

One of the most powerful blessings of covenant is the one-flesh relationship. When we are joined in marriage, God does a miracle. He takes two very different people and makes them one entity, *"one flesh."* The totality of what He does takes time to understand, but since this promise is repeated five times in the Scriptures (in Genesis, Malachi, Matthew, Mark and Ephesians), we know it is an important one.

Most couples view themselves as two individuals in a cohabitation. God, however, sees them as one single entity and encourages each partner *"in honor prefer one another"* (Romans 12:10). We are to love each other as ourselves. Therefore, we are to please each other in everything that we do and to be ready to make any necessary sacrifice for each other. Those who have not captured this reality are missing one of life's greatest blessings.

Only God can take two and make them one, but He can do it. He says nothing about whether you have made the right choice or not in a mate. He leaves that up to you. But, whether you have chosen well or not, God does the miracle of joining the two of you and making you one.

Each of us has a unique temperament and is not attracted to the same type of person of the opposite sex. God, therefore, gives us the privilege of making the choice of our lifetime partner. It is an important choice, and we should ask Him to guide us as we choose. As parents, Noline and I have prayed for our children, from the day they were born, that the right mate would come into their lives at the appropriate time. But we have also taught our children that when they have made their choice, and they are joined in marriage, it is for life. Therefore, their choice must be a Christ-centered one, one that has God's blessing, and their chosen spouse must be *"equally yoked"* (on the same spiritual level) with them.

But when the choice has been made and the joining process has begun, there is no turning back. The two are made *"one flesh,"* and no one has the right to separate them.

This miracle of God is a revelation for those who are looking to God for answers for their serious marital conflicts. There is no relationship that God cannot heal. There is no rift that He cannot bring back together. There is no problem that He cannot resolve.

Man makes marital problems seem impossible, and, indeed, some of them are serious; but God has always majored in doing the impossible. This is the reality that we must apply to our marital conflicts day by day. God can and will heal and restore any marriage, under any circumstances — if we will but give Him His rightful place as Lord of our lives. As Christians, we have no other alternative. No exit has been provided.

Noline and I are prime examples of the miracle of God. Our marriage was mortally wounded, and there seemed to be no hope for us. But God took two people who had lived the first twelve years of their marriage as "married singles," and He truly made us one. Once we gave Him the right to touch us in every area of our lives, even where it hurt, the miracle began to happen. Nobody who knows us today could imagine that we were once on the brink of divorce. God has done exactly what He promised to do.

Do we lose something by allowing God to make us one? Not at all. Just the opposite is true. We gain everything. Since God has put into us an attraction for those who are opposite to us, a shy one is often joined to a bold one, a mathematical genius sometimes joined to an art connoisseur, etc. In this way, God puts our strengths and weaknesses with others who also have different strengths and weaknesses, and where I may be lacking, my mate makes up for it. We are a well-designed team, not just gifted individuals, but a gifted unit. One of us might be able to *"chase a thousand,"* but the two of us together can *"put ten thousand to flight"* (Deuteronomy 32:30).

This understanding of the one-flesh relationship that God has designed for us is not restrictive at all, as some imagine. It is actually very freeing. It is like a well-constructed highway, straight and smooth. I can get into bumpy areas only if I get off the beaten path. Everything is smooth — as long as I stay on the prescribed course.

Traveling on this highway could never be miscon-strued as legalism. Yes, I can get off, if I want to. But why would I want to? It would be foolish even to contemplate. As a former Rhodesian, I could insist on driving in America to the left of the highway divide against the on-coming traffic. But why would I want to risk my life by doing that? It makes no sense. It is to my benefit to stay on this highway, just as it was designed by God. He knows what He is doing, and I cannot improve on His plan. If I agree to follow His ways, I will be blessed. That's enough for me to know. That is not legalism. That is not restrictive. That is not loss. That is all for my good, and I thank God for the privilege of driving here.

It does require a period of transition and retraining. When we first arrived in the States, friends picked us up at the airport and drove us around for a couple of weeks while we had studied the traffic laws and the traffic signs and felt sufficiently oriented to apply for a driving per-mit. Only after we had settled into our new home and begun to understand the traffic system, did we attempt to drive ourselves.

We felt a little foolish. After all, we had been legally driving in Africa for fourteen years before coming here, but it takes time to relearn everything and to adapt to un-familiar circumstances.

None of should feel badly about the need for relearn-ing everything. We are all in the same boat. Having lived for years in the world, and having been ingrained with its principles and laws, to unlearn everything we know and learn new ways from biblical truths takes time. Certain truths may take more study and prayer than others, but God will give the revelation if we are determined not to rely on the natural mind, or what we have been taught in the world.

The work of the Holy Spirit is to lead us into all truth, and when we give Him opportunity and maintain an open heart to receive, He will reveal to us the truths we need to move forward. Without His intervention we remain in darkness, with many wrong concepts that hinder us.

An American friend of ours went out to Zimbabwe some years ago to marry a girl he had met at Bible college. He had heard many stories about Africa and had seen movies of the jungles on "the dark continent," so he wasn't quite sure what he would find when he got there. It was late at night when his plane touched down, and all he could see around him were the outlines of dense bushes. What was out there among the bushes he could only imagine.

The family of the girl he had gone to marry met him, took him to their home, and put him in their camper for the night. But my friend couldn't sleep. All night long he heard the scratching of monkeys on the camper roof, and it made him very uneasy. He couldn't wait for daylight to come.

Early the next morning, when he was able to look out, my friend discovered that there were no monkeys at all.

Some branches from a bush had been blowing against the roof of the trailer and making the noise he heard. His preconceived ideas about Africa had produced in his mind the images of wild animals, when, in reality, none existed. He was in a well-developed residential area. These are the tricks the enemy plays on our minds, unless we experience a renewal of our thinking through God's intervention. Let us renew our minds through the work of Calvary so that we can have new understanding of God's will for each of us.

When we make a decision not to live like the world, that doesn't mean that we are giving up everything, as many imagine. When the Lord told His disciples not to be as others, He promised them a very different type of Kingdom:

> *And I confer on you a kingdom, just as my Father conferred one on me.* Luke 22:29

God never asks us to give up anything without replacing it with something far better. In the end, we are not giving up anything or missing anything. We are rather opting for the very best that God has to offer.

Forsaking the lifestyle of the world should not be a sad thing for any of us. What do we have to be sad about? God is giving us His very best. The blessings of living according to God's Kingdom principles not only assures us of a blessed life down here, but also of life everlasting. Therefore, with joy and anticipation, let us embrace the revelation of the *"one flesh"* God has destined us to be.

Understanding the One-Flesh Relationship

Some may say that this one-flesh concept sounds like an ideal that could take us a lifetime to learn. Well, however long it takes us to learn it, it is worth all the effort. So, do whatever you have to do to break loose from your old carnal thinking and let God help you take your marriage to a higher level of fulfillment.

CHAPTER FIVE

REPENTING AND FORGIVING

So watch yourselves. If your brother sins, rebuke
him, and if he repents, forgive him. If he sins against
you seven times in a day, and seven times comes
back to you and says, "I repent," forgive him.

Luke 17:3-4

There is no substitute for learning the principles of God's Kingdom, and the better we can learn those principles, the more freedom and fulfillment we will find in marriage. One of the first principles we must understand is the principle of repentance. This is a key that unlocks the door to God's Kingdom. What does it mean to repent?

Repentance represents a one-hundred-and-eighty-degree turn in our lives, a willingness to realize that we have been headed in the wrong direction and a readiness to take a new direction, God's direction.

In one sense, repentance represents total surrender, for when we decide to go God's way, we surrender all our own concepts and traditions and willingly accept His traditions and concepts. This may seem like loss to some, but His ways are so much better than our ways that we should be thrilled with the privilege of putting down the old to embrace the new. We should rejoice in putting down the lesser to accept the greater.

But repentance is not just a onetime thing. Although we are saved, we do not totally change overnight, and since it takes us time to unlearn the old and to learn the new, we must have a continued attitude of surrender to God, a continued sense of willingness to allow Him to have His way in our lives, a continued openness to His new and better thoughts.

Just as God responds readily to a repentant heart, a repentant heart also goes a long way to break down barriers in the marriage. When we feel that we know it all, that we have done nothing wrong, and that whatever problems exist must be the fault of our spouse, a hardness develops that prevents progress from being made. When, on the other hand, we consistently recognize that we are in the learning process, that we have had many wrong concepts, and that we have made plenty of mistakes ourselves, that softens the heart of our mates to bear with us while we learn God's ways and perfect the character of Christ in us. Repentance softens hearts and opens the way for new and fresh communication.

During the early years of our own marriage, when we still hadn't learned how to blend our strengths and weaknesses together in God's way, but rather continually saw our differences as a hindrance to individual progress, we made many mistakes, often selfishly pursuing our own ambitions, while ignoring the needs of the other. It was during this time that I allowed a passing interest in another woman in our congregation to develop into something much more serious. Before long, I had committed adultery with her and violated the vows of faithfulness I had made to my wife and to God, on our wedding day.

When I fell into adultery, my heart became very hardened, and nothing could penetrate it. It was only after I was able to repent of my sin, both to the Lord and to my wife, that I found my heart softening again. Once I had humbled myself before my wife and repented for my unfaithfulness, God was able to soften my heart, removing the hardness, and give me back a tenderness toward Him — and toward Noline as well.

Our world doesn't view adultery as being something serious. Rather it has become casual and rather commonplace in our society. Some "experts" even say that the marriage relationship may benefit from an occasional extramarital affair. But this is clearly not true. By committing adultery, I had stepped outside the bounds of God's Word and principles for marriage, and until I could repent of that violation and seek His forgiveness, my heart found no rest. There is no way that dabbling in darkness can enhance the relationship God envisions in marriage. Repentance paves the way back into full relationship with God, with the rest of the Body of Christ, and with your spouse and children.

Despite this fact, very little repentance is practiced publicly in the church, and this is a shame. Perhaps our lack of public repentance demonstrates a lack of private repentance. If we could repent more readily inside the home, perhaps we could find it more easy to do so before our fellow believers. This would not diminish us as individual believers or as leaders in the church. A little humility never hurt anyone.

Most Christians understand the concept of repentance as a necessary ingredient when we come to God seeking for His salvation, and they would never hesitate to mention repentance in this regard. But most Christians tend to overlook the need for repentance from that point on, feeling that to admit that they are less than perfect now somehow minimizes their salvation experience or brings ill repute upon the Lord or the church. This is just not true.

Have you never offended a fellow brother? Have you never thought or said something you were later sorry for? Have you never made a mistake of any kind? Of course you have. But mistakes are not fatal. If you are man enough or woman enough to recognize your wrong and ask the person you have offended to forgive you, no permanent damage is done to the relationship. People are forgiving — if you are repentant.

However, if you are one of those people who are sure that they always say and do the right thing and have never said or done anything offensive, you need to wake up and come to your senses. Your attitude is turning people off, and you will never have success in your relationship.

If we could just get Christian men and women to admit to their spouses that they were not perfect, and that they needed help, we could immediately cut the divorce rate in half. If people believe that you are conscious of your shortcomings and are working to correct them, they can be very patient with you. But when you refuse to accept the fact that you are the problem, what hope does that give them for the future? It is this attitude, more than anything else, that causes spouses to believe that their present relationship can never be healed. Repentance opens doors in relationships, and the lack of repentance closes them.

Another major principle of God's Kingdom, one that goes hand in hand with repentance, is forgiveness. When we repent, God is gracious to forgive us. And when others repent at having offended us, God expects us to be forgiving, in turn. When we are not willing to forgive, it is a slap in the face of God, a serious infraction of His laws and it is bound to have serious consequences. It is only when you release a person who has offended you that God releases you to move forward in your personal life. So, God expects you to forgive, even if there is no repentance from others.

Jesus' words to His disciples, in this regard, are notable. He said, *"So watch yourselves."* What could be more powerful? *WATCH YOURSELVES!* This is a serious matter.

Earlier in the chapter Jesus had warned that offenses would come, but that we should not be the offending party. He said:

> *It is impossible but that offences will come: but woe unto him, through whom they come! It were better for him that a millstone were hanged about his neck, and he cast into the sea, than that he should offend one of these little ones.*   Luke 17:1-2 (KJV)

63

It was then that Jesus said to His disciples, *"So watch yourselves."* His *"watch yourselves"* has two implications: First, we are to watch ourselves that we are not the offending party. But secondly, we are to watch ourselves that we are forgiving when our spouses offend us.

Offenses will come. None of us is perfect. We all make mistakes. We say things without thinking how it might sound to someone else. We do things that hurt each other, many times unintentionally. And we all expect others to recognize these facts and to be forgiving of us when we err. That's fine! But are we forgiving of others? The shoe is usually always on the other foot, for some reason. We are much too quick to judge and much too slow to forgive. This lack of forgiveness hinders our personal spiritual progress and the development of our potential in marriage.

How many times should we forgive a person who has offended us? Jesus answered that in this particular passage. He said that if a person offends you seven times in one day and ask you to forgive him seven times in that one day, you should forgive him seven times that day. On another occasion, when the disciples asked Him if seven times a day was the absolute limit, He said that we should even forgive *"seventy times seven"* (Matthew 18:22, KJV).

It is not for you to decide if a person deserves to be forgiven or not. If they repent, Jesus said, *"Forgive them."* If you make it optional, it will never get done. So it's not optional. It's a command. *Forgive them!* Again, even if they do not repent, we are still under a command to forgive.

Repenting and Forgiving

The disciples found this teaching rather alarming and wondered if their faith was great enough to allow them to comply with its far-reaching implications. *"Increase our faith,"* they cried. But Jesus insisted that their faith was sufficient for the task. "Just do it," He seemed to say.

All of us find it in ourselves to forgive — when the circumstances are right. All of us are willing to give others a chance — if they don't blow it again and again and again. But Jesus was saying that our willingness to forgive is a recognition of our own frailty and our need for Him to forgive us — over and over again. So we can't put limitations on it. We can't dictate the conditions. Forgive regardless of the sin. Forgive — regardless of the circumstances. Forgive — regardless of the frequency of the offense. You can do it, and you must.

It doesn't take a certified saint to show forgiveness. You don't need extraordinary faith in order to be forgiving. Forgive. Period!

Jesus refused to give His disciples any way out of this requirement. He refused to provide them with an escape clause. *"Forgive,"* He said. That's all.

There is no sin in your life too great that it cannot be forgiven by God, and there is no offense committed against you by your spouse that is so grievous that you cannot find it in your heart to forgive him or her. You don't have that option.

Jesus went on to tell the disciples about a faithful servant:

> *Suppose one of you had a servant plowing or looking after the sheep. Would he say to the servant when he*

65

*comes in from the field, "Come along now and sit
down to eat"? Would he not rather say, "Prepare
my supper, get yourself ready and wait on me while
I eat and drink; after that you may eat and drink"?
Would he thank the servant because he did what he
was told to do? So you also, when you have done everything you were told to do, should say, "We are
unworthy servants; we have only done our duty."*

Luke 17:7-10

Imagine it. The faithful servant worked all day in the
field, but when he came in from the field in the evening,
his work was not finished. He had to prepare his master's
meal and serve him before he could sit down himself and
have something. Yet, Jesus showed, he had done nothing
heroic or noteworthy. He had just done what was expected of servants. He had done his duty, and nothing
more.

And this entire teaching is related to forgiveness. Forgiving someone is not some heroic gesture that sets you
apart from all others and puts you in line for exceptional
praise. When you forgive, you have just done what is required of you, nothing more.

This seals our understanding of forgiveness. It is not
related to how we feel at the moment. It is not based on
how spiritual we may or may not be. It is a command,
and we are to obey it, regardless of any other circumstance or condition.

When I confessed my adulterous acts to Noline, she
had every reason to turn away from me. Her childhood
sweetheart had betrayed her. Some people advised her

that she should divorce me, and she considered it as a viable alternative. But she also knew the Scriptures and she knew that if she could not find it in her heart to forgive the wrong I had done to her, this failure would hinder her the rest of her life.

For a time, her pride and all the woundedness she received would not permit her to act on what she knew to be the right thing to do. Every wounded spouse wants to maintain some semblance of dignity and respect. And this desire often forces them to resist forgiveness much longer than they know they should. But Noline wanted God's blessings on her life, so she knew that ultimately she must forgive me. And this she did, as difficult as it was.

No matter how difficult it may be for a wounded spouse to forgive his or her partner, it must be done. Once the power of forgiveness is released, then the Lord begins to work on the heart of the offender. If there is no forgiveness, this process is delayed, and both parties are bound because of the sin — the original sin, and the sin of unforgiveness which complicates the situation.

Unforgiveness may be likened to a person who puts his hand into a fire and takes up a hot coal to throw at the one who has offended him. He only gets injured more in the process.

Forgiveness is like a giant nutcracker. It breaks the resistance of the offender and allows God to work on his heart. By refusing to forgive, you are placing yourself as an obstacle in God's way and preventing Him from doing His work.

Breaking Loose

You have a choice. You can either run a red light, or you can obey the laws and keep an orderly flow of traffic. The choice is yours.

By learning to repent when you are wrong and to forgive when you are wronged, you remove some of the greatest obstacles to happiness and you begin to break loose and to take your marriage to a higher level of fulfillment.

CHAPTER SIX

LOVING EACH OTHER — AS WE LOVE GOD

Master, which [is] the great commandment in the law? Jesus said unto him, thou shalt love the Lord thy God with all thy heart, and with all thy soul, and with all thy mind. This is the first and great commandment. And the second [is] like unto it, Thou shalt love thy neighbor as thyself.

Matthew 22:36-39 (KJV)

One of the most important reasons that God created men and women in His image was for fellowship. Man could communicate and relate to God in a manner the angels could not. And God knew that man would need His fellowship, just as He needed the fellowship of man. The highlight of Adam and Eve's day came when the three of them would meet in the garden. Man enjoyed the presence of his Creator, and God enjoyed the presence of His creation.

Relationship is always close to the heart of God. He requires that we love Him and that we love each other — in exactly the same way. It would seem that there is no need to speak to married people of love. After all, a marriage is the union of two people who love each other. But, with the passing of time, and the trials of life that come with it, the feeling of love often suffers. And the heart of God is grieved when we are not loving each other and demonstrating that love as He intended.

Drawing close to God does not always mean drawing closer to each other. For many years, Noline and I were serving God in the pastoral ministry, and we felt that because we were serving Him in this way, our personal relationship would automatically improve. We had been taught in Bible college that God becomes part of the marriage, a little like a love-triangle. He is at the top, and the husband and wife are at each corner of the base. The closer we got to God, we were assured, the closer we would come to each other. We found, however, that this was not true in our own relationship. Because our goals were different and we worked independently toward those goals, we were not growing closer to each other. We were actually growing further apart.

None of us would deny the fact that we are commanded to love our *neighbors* as ourselves, but the practicality of living it out from day to day, even in the marriage, is not always as easy as it sounds.

It is far easier to love God than it is to love our spouses. God doesn't burn the toast. He doesn't squeeze the toothpaste tube in the wrong place. He doesn't leave the toilet seat up or leave His clothes in the middle of the floor. And because we can't see Him, we think of Him in a totally different way. We love to get alone with God and have fellowship with Him because He affects our hearts, not our house; our lives, not our living room; our feelings, not our food. But God clearly wants us to learn to love each other in the same way that we love Him.

The Apostle John wrote to the churches:

> *If anyone says, "I love God," yet hates his brother, he is a liar. For anyone who does not love his brother, whom he has seen, cannot love God, whom he has not seen.* 1 John 4:20

It is wrong to say that you love God, while you hate others, sometimes even your own spouse. God could say that because if we really love Him, that love will be demonstrated in the way we treat those closest to us.

During our years of marital struggle, when Noline and I started arguing about something, my escape was to go to the office and pray or find a good book to read, or something else to take my mind off my problems. Noline was wise to my escape routine and sometimes called down the stairs as I was leaving: "Don't think that you can pray when you get into your office, because God won't hear your prayers." She was right. It isn't possible to get up from an argument with your spouse and begin worshiping God with sincerity and a clear conscience.

When we know that a brother has something against us, the Bible teaches, it is better to leave our place at the altar and make things right with that brother before we continue praying. Then, when we have come back, God will attend to our prayers.

Any of us who has had the experience knows that when you have been kind and loving and tender towards your spouse, and then you make your way into your prayer chamber and begin to worship the Lord, the atmosphere is totally different. The voice of the Lord breaks through and speaks into your heart and says, "I know you love Me, son." If you ask the question, "How do You know I love You, Lord?" He answers back, "Because you love your wife. This is a demonstration of your love for Me."

Learning this truth and implementing it in our marriage relationship has supernaturally connected us as a husband and wife in a new dimension of our love. We are seeing many answers to prayer because of this renewed sense of love for each other. God is pleased with our attitude and blesses it with answers from Heaven. When we can't seem to get an answer to our prayers, the first thing we check is the status of our relationship as husband and wife. If we have allowed something, anything, to come between us — our finances, our children, our ministry — we deal with that thing and get it out of the way, because we know that it is a hindrance to our prayers, as the Scriptures show:

> *Husbands, in the same way be considerate as you live with your wives, and treat them with respect as the weaker partner and as heirs with you of the gracious gift of life, so that nothing will hinder your prayers.*   1 Peter 3:7

Once we have patrolled the hedges of our personal lives, if we have found any holes in the fence where the enemy is getting a foothold, we go to battle against the devil and close off any place of opportunity that he might otherwise use to gain some foothold in our home. We know that if we maintain a home that is impervious to enemy attack, we will do well. And love shared and demonstrated presents an impenetrable wall against satanic attack.

Developing a lifestyle of loving each other, and thus demonstrating our love for God, is not always easy. In our case, Noline and I are total opposites in temperament. I am a morning person, while she is a night person. I am more of an administrator and a visionary, whereas Noline is more motivated toward showing mercy and giving. It takes a lot of time and energy on our part, talking and praying together, for God to take our strengths and weaknesses and blend them together to produce the desired unity in our relationship. And if we didn't allow this to happen, those differences would divide us and dilute our love for each other.

Jesus demonstrated His love for the Father through total obedience, and His love for all mankind, by laying His life down for the world. There could be no greater demonstration of love. Therefore the Scriptures declare:

> *Greater love has no one than this, that he lay down his life for his friends.* John 15:13

When Jesus showed His love for us in this way, He was showing His love for His heavenly Father.

As partners in the God-inspired relationship called marriage, we have an obligation to God to love one another, in the same way Christ loved us:

Husbands, love your wives, just as Christ loved the church and gave himself up for her to make her holy, cleansing her by the washing with water through the word, and to present her to himself as a radiant church, without stain or wrinkle or any other blemish, but holy and blameless. In this same way, husbands ought to love their wives as their own bodies. He who loves his wife loves himself. After all, no one ever hated his own body, but he feeds and cares for it, just as Christ does the church — for we are members of his body. "For this reason a man will leave his father and mother and be united to his wife, and the two will become one flesh." This is a profound mystery — but I am talking about Christ and the church. However, each one of you also must love his wife as he loves himself, and the wife must respect her husband. Ephesians 5:25-33

This entire teaching is based on Christ's actions on that fateful Passover night and His trip to Calvary the next day. His willingness to give Himself was His demonstration of love, and God requires that we love each other in this same unselfish way.

One year, we were asked to do communion for our Marriage Ministries International Conference in Denver. In preparation for that role, I read many related scriptures and spent some time praying and meditating on the subject, trying to see the experience from God's perspective. One of the passages I read was this:

For I received from the Lord what I also passed on to

Loving Each Other — As We Love God

you: The Lord Jesus, on the night he was betrayed,
took bread, and when he had given thanks, he broke
it and said, "This is my body, which is for you; do
this in remembrance of me."
In the same way, after supper he took the cup, say-
ing, "This cup is the new covenant in my blood; do
this, whenever you drink it, in remembrance of me."
For whenever you eat this bread and drink this cup,
you proclaim the Lord's death until he comes.

                                    1 Corinthians 11:23-26

While I was sitting in the car waiting for Noline to finish some shopping one day (and it seemed like I had been
waiting a long time), God suddenly began to speak to me.
First, He reminded me of His words, *"Do this ... in remem-*
brance of Me." Then, He showed me that we were missing
the point of His *"do this."* I was left to meditate on what
this could mean. I could hardly wait to get home and re-
study all the scriptures on communion. I even looked up
the word in the dictionary. It said:

> *Communion: a sharing; possession in common;*
> *sharing of one's thoughts and emotions; an intimate*
> *spiritual relationship; celebrating of the Eucharist.*

The last definition, "celebrating of the Eucharist," is
more of a function, whereas the first three are relational. I
suddenly came to believe that, through the communion,
Jesus wanted us to understand the commitment of following Him. He wanted to say to every one of us, "All of
Me or nothing." He had said:

75

Breaking Loose

I am the living bread that came down from heaven. If anyone eats of this bread, he will live forever. This bread is my flesh, which I will give for the life of the world. John 6:51

I had to read all of the sixth chapter of John again before the full impact of what He was saying hit me. We have always thought of the communion as the last supper, but now I saw that very early in the book of John Jesus was laying a foundation, so that we would not later misinterpret His instructions. What He was saying was that we should be willing to give ourselves, in the same way He was willing to give Himself.

As I read over the related Scriptures again, a new excitement came into my soul, and I sensed that the Holy Spirit was guiding me. After studying all of those passages, I again came to the conclusion that although the disciples were to eat the bread and drink the cup, what Christ was asking them to *do* was exactly what He was about to *do*, to give His life for the world.

Most churches celebrate the Lord's table, providing the bread and the cup, to be taken in remembrance of what Christ has done for us. And this is altogether fitting. He was totally committed and dedicated to His mission, and in the end, He went to Calvary, taking upon Himself the sins of the whole world. This sacrifice must not be minimized in any way.

As we partake of the emblems of the communion service, we should appropriate the finished work of Calvary to our spiritual and physical lives. Jesus took my sin and, in its place, gave me His righteousness. If there is any righteousness in me, therefore, it is because of His sacrifice. If there is any victory in my life, all the glory is due unto Him. Paul wrote:

We are more than conquerors through him who loved us. Romans 8:37

Let us appropriate all that He has provided for us through the cross. But, at the same time, let us not miss the point of Jesus' teachings. What is it that we are to *do*? As Christ expressed the fullness of His love by giving Himself, we must learn to lay ourselves down for others, as an honest expression of our love for God and the resulting love we feel for others.

Jesus is our example. As He has given Himself for us, and thus demonstrated the fullness of His love, we must give ourselves for each other. In this way, we show that we truly love Him. Most of the original disciples gave their lives for the sake of the Gospel, showing us that they accepted the Lord's challenge.

For many, if not most Christians, the communion has become far too symbolic and is taken far too lightly. John, one of the disciples who was present that night, would later write:

This is how we know what love is: Jesus Christ laid down his life for us. And we ought to lay down our lives for our brothers. 1 John 3:16

The power of the communion commitment is further revealed as Paul went on to say:

Breaking Loose

For anyone who eats and drinks without recognizing the body of the Lord eats and drinks judgment on himself. That is why many among you are weak and sick, and a number of you have fallen asleep. But if we judged ourselves, we would not come under judgment. When we are judged by the Lord, we are being disciplined so that we will not be condemned with the world.   1 Corinthians 11:29-32

Before we take communion, we should examine ourselves, and if we judge ourselves properly, we will not come into judgment later. Are we remembering what Christ did for us on Calvary? And are we ready to lay our lives down in the same way? Are we demonstrating our love for God by loving those around us? Those who are only fooling themselves, said Paul, are in danger of becoming weak and sickly or even of dying.

Since the day God gave us this revelation, when Noline and I take communion together, we take advantage of the opportunity to do an examination of our lives together. "Am I laying my life down for you daily?" I ask. If the answer is positive, then I feel free to partake of the bread. If I determine that I have not been fulfilling my responsibility toward Noline, I repent and ask her to forgive me, and only then do I feel free to partake — when I have made a proper judgment.

"Am I willing to shed my blood for you?" I ask. And, again, if I can answer yes to that question, then we feel ready to partake of the cup.

Regularly taking the communion helps us make the

transition from darkness to light, from selfishness to selflessness, from worldly attitudes to Kingdom attitudes.

If I want to have a successful marriage, I must die to the old ideas of self-gratification and start living for the needs of my spouse, in honor preferring her. Only then can I expect to break loose from the chains of mediocrity that have bound me and to be free to love my spouse the way God intended. And, in doing so, I am showing the world that I love God. This is being a role model for others to follow.

Grasping the importance of loving each other as we love God enables us to break loose and to take our marriages to a higher level of fulfillment.

CHAPTER SEVEN

LEARNING TO LIVE TOGETHER IN UNITY

*How good and pleasant it is when brothers live to
gether in unity!*
*It is like precious oil poured on the head, running
down on the beard,*
running down on Aaron's beard,
down upon the collar of his robes.
*It is as if the dew of Hermon were falling on Mount
Zion.*
*For there the LORD bestows his blessing, even life
forevermore.*   Psalms 133:1-3

Many years ago, when Noline and I were struggling in our marriage relationship, we requested prayer one day from a visiting pastor. As he was praying over us, he sensed the Holy Spirit speaking to him in a word picture for us. This word picture was of the face of a clock, with its two hands. He was led to pray that like the two hands of a clock that are facing in different directions yet working together to tell the true time, God would bring the two of us into a meaningful cadence, a miraculous unity for our personal lives and for our ministry.

He saw that, in order to achieve this unity, we would have to get in step with God, and that it would seem to others that we were out of step with them. We could not live as other couples, if we chose to have unity in our relationship; for that unity only comes from God and from obeying God. We had no idea how God would answer that prayer, but we were believing that He would.

Not long afterward we attended a Married For Life marriage course where we were taught principles that we began to apply to our own lives. This was the open door from which God could deepen our relationship. Until then, as we have said, we had been living as married singles. I had been pursuing my goals in ministry, and Noline had been pursuing her goals in being a wife and mother. We were not walking in cadence with each other, in any sense of the word. Learning and applying those biblical principles turned our lives around completely and brought about the beginnings of a unity we had only imagined before. Unity is possible in the marriage relationship, when we are willing to do things God's way.

The couple that God placed in the Garden of Eden, His picture of the perfect marriage, were in harmony with each other and with their Maker. They were free to enjoy the Garden of Eden, to enjoy each other's presence, and to relax in the presence of God *"in the cool of the day."* This is not just an idyllic impossibility. This is the harmony and tranquility that God intended for marriage.

The fact that man fell and was driven from the Garden does not mean that unity in the marriage relationship is forever lost. When Jesus died on the cross, He not only redeemed our souls from sin and death, He also redeemed our marriages to the full blessing and freedom that Adam and Eve enjoyed in the Garden. It is not impossible to be one in spirit and mind, and God expects us to work toward that end.

God has ordained a unity of sorts between all believers. Jesus prayed that His followers would enjoy the same oneness He had with the Father. This unity, the psalmist showed us, is *"good"* and *"pleasant"* in the sight of God. Unity is *"good and pleasant,"* just as disunity is not good and not pleasant. Strife injected into any situation turns that situation into something altogether different. And when strife exists between the partners in a marriage, life suddenly takes on a totally different perspective, where even small tasks become difficult.

When two people are in unity, they can tackle even big problems with perseverance, and they prevail. There is strength in unity, and there is weakness in dissention.

It is interesting that God uses the illustration of Aaron when speaking about the unity He desires among brothers. Aaron was the first high priest and, as such, the man who stood between the people and their Maker. Anointing oil was poured over him during the ceremony of consecration to the priesthood, and that oil represented the Holy Spirit and the peace and unity He brings to any life.

Aaron's responsibilities in the Tabernacle were defined by God at Mt. Sinai. He was not just to do his own thing. There was a prescribed method to everything he did, and God required him to perform his duties without error. When those duties were carried out according to the detailed instructions given to his brother Moses, there was peace and harmony in the camp.

Breaking Loose

Moses received the directives from God and gave them to Aaron. He was to begin at the Altar of Sacrifice, where an animal was to be slaughtered to present to God. Aaron was then to make his way to the Brazen Laver where he would cleanse himself after the sacrifice was completed. He would also change his outer garments and put on clean garments so that he was worthy to enter the Holy Place. Once inside the Holy Place, Aaron attended to the Candlestick to make sure it was burning properly and that it was full of oil. Next, he placed bread on the Show Table, symbolizing the manna the Lord had provided for His people in the wilderness. Then Aaron poured a carefully mixed incense onto the Altar of Incense. The aroma of it would drift upward, as a pleasing sacrifice of acceptable worship to the Lord.

Once a year Aaron was to go into the Holy of Holies, taking with him the blood of a spotless lamb. He would sprinkle that blood on the Ark of the Covenant and, if God accepted the sacrifice, the sins of the people would be forgiven for the past year.

It became the custom of the people of Israel to gather around the Tabernacle during these sacrifices. The day's events were so important to the well-being of them all that they watched with anticipation.

If the sacrifice had been accepted by God, the people would know — when they saw the Shekinah glory of God descending on the Holy of Holies. If that glory appeared, great shouts of victory would go up from the crowd, for forgiveness, peace, and unity with God would be proclaimed for another year.

That proclamation was not always made. If the high

priest had not been faithful to God, if he had conducted himself in some way that was displeasing to God, or if the sacrifice was blemished in any way, not only would the sacrifice not be accepted, and the Shekinah glory would not descend, but the high priest himself would be smitten there in the presence of God and die. Because of this fact, each high priest had a rope attached to his ankle when he went into the Holy of Holies. Should he fail and his offering be rejected, the people could pull his body out for proper burial. This was serious business.

We have come to discover that the single most destructive force in any relationship is the choice not to do the right thing, not to obey God's directives concerning marriage. This rebellion against God not only brings with it a personal death, it has the power to rob the marriage of its God-ordained blessings. Obedience always brings life, and disobedience always brings death.

Aaron became a symbol of unity because he obeyed God, and his obedience brought God's blessing upon the entire nation of Israel. Peace and harmony for all began with the obedience of a single individual.

In the light of this teaching, it is easy to see why marriage is so chaotic today, for every individual wants to do his or her own thing. We each want the benefits of marriage, but, at the same time, we want to continue enjoying the freedom of the single life. So what do we expect?

Blessings always come down from above. Therefore, to have blessings upon our marriage, we need to learn to obey God's Word. It is time that we stop trying to put our particular interpretation on the guidelines God has set up for us, and simply start obeying them.

Breaking Loose

But experiencing unity is not a onetime act. We must consistently work at it. Paul wrote to the Ephesians:

> *Make every effort to keep the unity of the Spirit through the bond of peace.*   Ephesians 4:3

Achieving this unity requires an *"effort."*

What does it mean to *"keep the unity of the Spirit"*? It means that we must obey the voice of the Spirit, when He speaks to us, doing what He has indicated. Once we have heard His voice, regardless of the issues involved, it is time for obedience. None of us is perfect in this regard.

Once, when Noline and I were flying back from the Caribbean Islands to Denver, one of our layovers was in the Dallas-Fort Worth International Airport. We had about an hour and a half layover there, and while we were waiting at that very busy place, Noline went off to find a rest room. While she was gone, I was thinking to myself how nice it would be if I could get our tickets upgraded to first class. I had heard other people talking about going to the counter and asking for upgrades and getting them, without any extra cost. I decided it was worth a try. What did we have to lose?

I waited in line until it was my turn and then asked if there were any available seats in first class, as I would like to upgrade. The lady said there were and that she would change our tickets immediately. But now I had second thoughts. Just before my turn had come, I had sensed the Spirit saying to me, "Don't do it," so I was sure there would be no seats available. Now, what should I do?

Learning to Live Together In Unity

Before I got up my courage to say anything, the lady had gone off to change the tickets, and, after a while, she returned with new tickets. Handing them to me, she surprised me by saying, "How would you like to pay for this, Sir?"

Suddenly, I realized what I had done. I had not specified that I was seeking a free upgrade, and she had taken it for granted that I wanted to pay for the privilege. Well, it was too late now to admit my error. The tickets were already written. So I got out my credit card and paid the extra fare. Now I was wondering what I was going to say to Noline.

When I saw her walking toward me, I got up immediately, and before she could say anything, I said, "Just say you forgive me." Obviously she wanted to know what she was forgiving me for, but I insisted, "No, just say that you forgive me." So she said, "Okay, I forgive you. Now, what did you do?" When I explained to her about the first class upgrade and how I had to pay for it, she was visibly angry and told me that I had to take the tickets back immediately and get our money reimbursed. We didn't need to fly first class, and we didn't need to be wasting money on that luxury.

My pride would not let me go back to that counter and ask an agent to refund our money and change our tickets back again, so I took out Noline's ticket and handed it to her and told her that if she wanted to change it, she could go do it herself. This made her even more angry, so I started to walk off. When I did this, she started praying out in a loud voice.

I was embarrassed that my wife, an introvert, was

praying so loud that everyone could hear her in a busy airport. I rushed back to her and said, "It's okay to pray, but just pray quietly." We prayed together quietly for a few minutes.

During that time of prayer the Lord spoke to my heart to repent for not obeying the voice of the Spirit, when He had told me not to change the ticket. I did that, and I repented to my wife for allowing my pride to bring strife into our relationship.

Noline also repented for her attitude. And, once we had resolved the strife, we were able to talk rationally about the tickets. In the end, she forgave me, and we were back to having unity in our relationship. We flew home first class.

Staying in unity with the Spirit necessitates that we hear what He is saying, and that we obey. I had broken that unity. I distinctly heard what He said, but I was too full of pride and too zealous to fly first class to obey. The disunity this created not only affected me, but also my wife and our relationship.

Our experience in the Dallas-Fort Worth Airport may have been a small thing, but it is the accumulation of many small things in our lives that eventually builds into a mountain that divides us. Each small thing must be dealt with on its own if we are to experience the Shekinah glory of God descending upon our relationship.

Disobedience, even in little things, grieves the Spirit of God:

And do not grieve the Holy Spirit of God ... .

Ephesians 4:30

Learning to Live Together In Unity

Just as Aaron was required to do exactly as he had been instructed, we too need to obey what we are taught of the Holy Spirit. When we have learned to obey in the small things, it is easy to obey in the larger issues.

God's desire is to see a larger *"unity of the faith"*:

> *To prepare God's people for works of service, so that the body of Christ may be built up until we all reach unity in the faith and in the knowledge of the Son of God and become mature, attaining to the whole measure of the fullness of Christ.* Ephesians 4:12-13

The Greek phrase translated here as *the unity of the faith* means "the conviction of the truth of anything, belief in God, in Christ, or the religious beliefs of Christians; fidelity and faithfulness." In context, then, the verse means, "staying in harmony with whom and what you believe."

The ministries of the apostle, the prophet, the evangelist, the pastor, and the teacher were all placed in the Body of Christ to bring us to full maturity, so that we can enjoy the unity that God has for us through the Holy Spirit.

Once we have been taught, however, a conscious effort is needed on the part of each individual, so that we can stay in harmony with each other. It is not enough to know what is needed. We must make the effort necessary to bring it to pass. You have to live what you believe.

If I believe in my heart that I should pray with my wife on a daily basis, then to stay in harmony with that belief, I must pray with her every day. If I believe that tithing is a biblical principle, then in keeping with what I believe, I must tithe. If I believe that God has called me to discipline my children, then in keeping with what I believe, I must guide them into a disciplined life-style that they may grow up as godly children before the Lord. And, since we believe that divorce is not pleasing to God, in keeping with what we believe, we have chosen never to use that threat against each other.

The principles of God are not grievous. They are for our benefit. Therefore, it is for the good of every one of us to be obedient to what He tells us. And if we expect to enjoy the fruit of God's presence and the blessing of His guidance in our marriage, then both of us must live what we believe together.

Far too many couples go to the altar of the church, asking God for a miracle in their relationship and then are not willing to obey what God tells them. If you have dug deep holes in your relationship and can't seem to get out, there is hope. God can turn your situation around.

As we have already seen in chapter five, repentance is the key. The first thing couples need to do is to repent of their willfulness or selfishness:

> *Remember, therefore, what you have received and heard; obey it, and repent.*   Revelation 3:3

> *Remember the height from which you have fallen! Repent and do the things you did at first.*
> Revelation 2:5

You can get back everything the devil has stolen from your relationship by going back and doing *"the things you did at first."* Can you remember how you courted each other, how you were kind and considerate to each other? Repent of your backsliding and go back and do those same things again, and God will do a work in your hearts. He will restore you to unity, and even bring you to a level of unity you never imagined possible.

One of the elements that most destroys unity in marriage is the unwillingness of one or both parties to be totally transparent with each other. We have come to regard this as one of the major keys to healing a relationship and of taking it to a new level of fulfillment. John wrote to the churches:

> *If we walk in the light as he is in the light, we have fellowship with one another and the blood cleanses us from all sin.* 1 John 1:5-7

Transparency produces fellowship, both with God and with each other. James confirmed this teaching:

> *Confess your sins to each other and pray for each other so that you may be healed.* James 5:16

The healing of which James spoke includes forgiveness and reconciliation. If there are dark and hidden areas of our lives that we are unwilling to share with our spouses and with God, if we have so many skeletons in the closet that we are afraid to open it up, for fear of what might pop out, we continually give Satan room to attack our relationship.

There is no other way around it. If we want to be

healed in our relationship, we must become vulnerable before each other.

Light is the principal characteristic of the Kingdom of God. So if our lives are full of darkness and secrecy and hidden actions, something is terribly wrong, and we will never enjoy all the benefits of the Kingdom. Children of light cannot spend their time in the darkness, and if there is darkness in us, we need to get rid of it — just as quickly as possible.

When Satan attacked Adam and Eve, he didn't do it while they were together. He knew that they would strengthen each other and help each other, so he came to Eve when she was alone. If she had brought her temptation to the attention of God and the attention of her husband, she could have overcome it. This is a secret we all need to learn.

Once Eve had responded and succumbed to the temptation and caused Adam to succumb to the temptation, the both of them made another classic mistake. They hid from God. The wonderful fellowship they had enjoyed was broken, because of the darkness that had come into the relationship through sin. They had disobeyed God, and they would now pay the consequences for their selfishness. Someone has said that the five major reasons for the breakup of every marriage are: (1) selfishness, (2) selfishness, (3) selfishness, (4) selfishness, and (5) selfishness, and I believe they were right.

This problem could have been resolved if Eve had immediately confessed to Adam what was happening with her and if the two of them had immediately called on God for His help. Over a period of time, however, the thing they were doing, came to seem good to them. Marriages cannot exist in harmony and unity if either the wife or the husband has a closet full of skeletons. We must be completely honest with each other.

We have been taught that confession can wound the spouse deeply and should be avoided, but it is the sin that has already been committed that wounds the relationship. Confession brings healing. Keeping the sin hidden only complicates recovery.

Undoubtedly, the single most difficult thing I ever had to do was to confess adultery to my wife. If I had known that confession would bring release, it would have been easier. But I had been counseled by men of God to confess only to Him and then to be quiet and never mention my sin again — to anyone. "After all," goes the argument, "if God buries my sins in the deepest sea, why should I bring them up again?"

Listening to my confession may have been the most difficult thing Noline ever had to do as well. To know that her childhood sweetheart had been unfaithful to her cut deeply, but once everything was out in the light, healing began to come to our marriage. It wasn't confession that wounded our marriage, it was the adultery. The confession started the healing process. It seems like a most difficult decision to make, but if you want total unity in your marriage there is no other way.

Noline and I long ago made the decision that we didn't want anything standing between us. With all of our hearts, we wanted God to make us *"one flesh,"* and this demanded that we hold back nothing from each other. This truth set us free.

Breaking Loose

"The unity of the faith" is not just believing the statement of faith of your particular church. It is a harmony of purpose and intent with the people around you, and it enables you to face the obstacles that arise, knowing that you have a shared goal in life. This unity begins with one person, for each of us must be obedient to God first as individuals, if we are to succeed as partners and as brothers in the larger community of believers.

This unity is *as if the dew of Hermon were falling on Mount Zion.* Hermon is always snow covered, and starting from the peak, the melting snow begins to flow downward. The first trickles become a small stream, and, slowly those small streams merge to become a great river, the mighty Jordan, that waters the surrounding valley and eventually winds its way into the Lake of Galilee. In all the areas traversed by the river, fruits are grown in abundance.

When one person walks in obedience to the Spirit of God, a small stream of blessing is formed. When stream is joined to stream, a mighty force is unleashed which is capable of bringing life and blessing to all those around it. That wonderful result is sure. The psalmist promised: *"For there the LORD bestows his blessing, even life forevermore."*

Start doing the things that bring unity to marriage and avoiding those things that divide you and you will experience a breaking loose and be able to take your marriage to a higher level of fulfillment.

CHAPTER EIGHT

AVOIDING A BREAKDOWN OF COMMUNICATIONS

*Casting down imaginations, and every high thing
that exalteth itself against the knowledge of God,
and bringing into captivity every thought to the obedience of Christ ...* 2 Corinthians 10:5-6 (KJV)

The Bible emphatically states that storms will come to our lives and warns us to prepare for those storms. Jesus showed that those who fail to heed this warning are in danger of seeing their house collapse.

Married life usually always starts off with a period in which both husband and wife are so infatuated with each other that they are blind to each other's faults. However, this honeymoon period always comes to an end, the rose-colored glasses come off, and we are sometimes shocked by what we see and wonder how we got ourselves into such a situation. It is at these critical times that communication between husband and wife is so important. Yet, communication, as many have learned, is one of the areas that most suffers when the marriage is being pummeled by the storms of life. Why is it that communication seems to break down just when we need it?

Breaking Loose

The simplest answer is that we each have our pride and self esteem to keep intact, and when we don't know how to face a certain situation, it is just easier not to say anything. This is a tragic mistake, however, because when we fail to talk and pray through small problems that arise early in the marriage, they invariably accumulate to cause a blowup somewhere along the line. I also believe that something much more important is at work. I have come to believe that when we stop communicating it is because we have begun to harden our hearts against each other.

Probably no one walks down the aisle on their wedding day thinking that they will try marriage out for a year or two and then divorce. Most people who marry truly expect that it will last a lifetime. So what does happen in a relationship where after two and three years of marriage the couples are heading for the divorce courts? The process is a slow one, but it always has the same tragic end. For a marriage to succeed in today's world, it is essential for the husband and wife to communicate on a regular basis.

You must make time to talk to each other, changing other appointments, if necessary, to fit in the most important person in your life, outside of God: your spouse. Even children, who are the product of an intimate relationship, are secondary to the importance of maintaining health in the one-flesh relationship.

When we allow a breakdown of communication, the result is a growth of all sorts of imaginations. "Maybe he doesn't really love me." "Maybe he never did." "Maybe she prefers the company of others more than mine." A

Avoiding A Breakdown Of Communications

simple conversation and the humbling of the heart would and could eliminate such vain imaginations.

Anything at all can be an excuse for hardening our hearts against our loved ones. As an example:

I had an old motorcycle that had no starter. It had to be kick-started. One day I was trying to start it, but the battery was low, so no matter how many times I tried to kick-start the cycle, it just wouldn't work. Finally, I got a great idea. I would tie a rope to the motorcycle and to the back of our car, then have Noline pull me slowly down the road so that I could jump-start the bike.

I told Noline what I wanted to do. When she got up to 10 or 20 m.p.h., I would put the bike in second gear, let out the clutch, and start the motor. I would then motion to her with my hand so that she could see in the rearview mirror that the bike was started, and she could stop. She agreed.

I tied the bike behind the car, and we started off down the road. When Noline had gotten up a little speed, I popped the clutch and, sure enough, the engine roared into life. I waved to Noline to let her know that she could stop now, but somehow she didn't see me and kept on going, even faster. I waved frantically to her, but couldn't get her attention, or maybe she thought I was telling her to go faster, for now she sped off, yanking the motorcycle into the air. I flew off the bike, landing on my head and shoulder on the blacktop. The motorcycle landed on its side and was dragged half a block more before Noline realized what had happened and that I was no longer following her.

This little episode would not have been half so bad if it

hadn't happened on Saturday, when most of our neighbors were home from work and were outside mowing their lawns and clipping their hedges. I was so embarrassed, and somehow, that day, I came to believe that women don't have a very good grasp of how mechanical things really work. Surely anyone could understand the simple procedure of an engine turning over and generating enough electrical power to start the engine — anyone except my wife, that is. And a seed of hardness grew from that moment, until I found myself not even willing to discuss mechanical things with Noline. I was even annoyed with her if she tried to initiate conversation on the topic. I had, in a very small but real way locked her out of that area of my life.

That one little incident was not enough to cause us to divorce or separate, but if we leave such conflicts untreated, they feed on themselves and become something much more menacing and dangerous.

Before I learned to be open with my wife in everything, I would resort to the usual tactics: ignoring her, cutting her out of my life, treating her like some stranger. If left unchecked, such conflicts can easily grow into the kind of struggle that separates even the best of friends. The day I realized that attitude was a threat to our relationship as a couple and began to deal with it once and for all was memorable to us both as husband and wife.

Gradually I learned that God's Kingdom dictates that I walk in softness and tenderness toward my wife, even when I don't understand her. There is no reason for me to shut her out of my world. I simply can't afford to do it.

Adultery begins with just such a seed. Men and women

alike are drawn, at times, to someone other than their spouses, when they feel that another person understands them better or appreciates them more. It doesn't happen because a husband or wife woke up one morning and decided to go out and have sex with someone else. It happens because men and women are not taking time to understand each other's viewpoints or they fail to understand where the other one is coming from on a certain subject.

An attraction to someone else other than your mate begins in a very small, seemingly insignificant, area where Satan knows you are vulnerable, but it happens because you have permitted a breakdown of communications and have done nothing to restore the damage.

The same can be said for abusive relationships. They often result because a person has built up a lot of hurts in his heart, and has not released them. They are released, instead, though violent acts, rather than through prayer and communication. We will look more fully into this issue in a later chapter on dealing with abuse.

At one point, God began to speak to me from that passage in the book of Malachi. At the close of Malachi's teaching about how God hates divorce, I found the very strong statement, *"So guard yourself in your spirit."*

God wants to make us one through the process of commitment and dedication, and the goal is *"godly offspring,"* children who love the Lord and are willing to serve Him. The key to this process is to *"guard ... your spirit."* Your situation can never come to divorce — unless you allow your heart to become hardened. That first slap in the face can never take place — if you refuse to allow your heart to be hardened.

When the slaps begin and the divorce papers appear, it is usually because no one is listening. Meaningful communication has ceased. Long ago their hearts were hardened and their ears were closed to anything anyone wants to say — even God. They are no longer in harmony with what they believe and no longer in unity with the Spirit. There is no repentance and no forgiveness.

God's teachings on divorce and abuse are sandwiched around His command "*guard ... your spirit.*" It is so important that it is repeated twice in this short passage. It is a lack in your spiritual life that is causing you to have problems performing sexually with your partner. It is a lack in your spiritual life, and the fact that you are full of anger and unforgiveness, that refuses to allow you to consider the feelings of your mate. You simply must deal with the issues that are destroying your spiritual life, through healthy conversation and prayer, or your marriage will not survive.

When the Holy Spirit first spoke to me from this passage, I didn't fully understand what He meant by "*take heed to your spirit*" (KJV). We had been taught in Bible college that when you don't understand a particular passage, you should just set it on the back burner and wait for God to reveal its meaning to you. So that's what I did.

Several months later, when we were doing a seminar at a retreat center in the Blue Hills of Pennsylvania, this principle became real to me. Noline and I were the special speakers of the morning, and we had determined to teach on spiritual warfare, showing those who attended the conference that we must use all the tools God has provided us to do battle against the enemy who is constantly attacking us. I had decided that I would wear work clothes — some old jeans, a T-shirt, sneakers and a ball cap — to show that we had to *work* at defeating our enemy.

I got up early and prepared myself and was chafing at the bit to get into the hall before the nine o'clock start time and get things started. When Noline still wasn't ready at eight forty-five, I asked her to please hurry. The meeting would be starting in fifteen minutes, and we needed to be there.

When nine o'clock arrived, I knew the meeting would be starting, and since Noline was still not ready to go, I started to get very upset with her. Noline knows that I like to be punctual and that being on time for my commitments is very important to me. I couldn't understand why she wasn't honoring that now. Something started rising in the pit of my stomach and moving slowly upward, and the longer she took to get ready, the higher the anger rose in me. By nine-fifteen, I was so upset that my anger was distorting my thinking, and by nine-twenty, I was raising my voice and making some heated accusations.

"Why are we always late for our meetings?

"You always make us late.

"Why is it that you are never ready on time?

"Why don't you plan your day better and get your clothes ready the night before?"

Statements like these, which, because of the anger of

the moment, come out in a very accusing manner, can be very damaging to the relationship — if they are not properly dealt with. Many unwise things are said when we are angry, most of them probably not true or not totally true, and they don't reflect what is in our hearts. But unless these thing can be clarified at some point, they will be believed and stored away for future use by our partners.

Noline was finally ready, and we rushed to the meeting. Before we entered the worship hall, however, she said to me, "I think you should take off the ball cap."

I thought to myself, *Why is she saying this now? She knows I plan to use it as part of my presentation.* So I said to her, "If God wants to speak to me, He can get through this thin layer of cloth on my ball cap."

This only escalated the conflict, and I sensed that Noline was about to use some scripture on me. She shot back, "You might offend someone if you keep it on during the worship service."

I know where she pulled that one from, I thought, *Luke 17:1-2.* I'm not going to be intimidated by her use of the Bible. But somehow I sensed that she was going to stand her ground and that she was telling me that it would be better for me if a millstone were tied around my neck and I was cast into the sea than to offend one of the *"little ones"* present at the conference.

I was so upset that I couldn't consider what she was saying and felt that I had to go her one better if I was to win this battle. I declared with intensity, "You have a religious spirit."

"I don't care," she said, "just remove the cap!"

With that, I ripped the cap off my head, screwed it up

into a small ball, and stuffed it into my back pocket. As we entered the meeting hall, we were not only not talking to each other, we were making sure not to touch each other. Once inside, I turned my back slightly from Noline and raised my hands in worship to the Lord, trying to get my thoughts together for the message we were about to give.

No sooner had I closed my eyes to focus on the Lord than the Holy Spirit began to speak to my heart. He asked me if I remembered the scripture in Malachi which I had read a few weeks earlier? I did, and the Holy Spirit proceeded to convict me of "closing my Spirit" toward my wife when things did not go my way. He showed me that I had been doing this to people since childhood and told me that by doing this I was guilty of several things: I was hardening my heart toward Noline and, at the same time, toward God. This was against the covenant vows I had made to my wife, and I needed to come under the Word that governs marriage. My actions represented the spirit of divorce and abuse already at work in my heart.

Secondly, it forced Noline to become oversensitive to my attitudes and caused her to perform for my acceptance.

"How would you feel," the Spirit asked me, "if your heavenly Father treated you the same way?" He ended this dialogue with me by saying that God hated this attitude.

To me, the only issue had been Noline's insensitivity to my desire to be on time and keep a commitment, but it now appeared that, although Noline was certainly wrong to make us late for that important meeting, I was even more wrong to close my spirit to her and to risk damaging our relationship.

Right there, totally oblivious to my surroundings, I turned to Noline and told her that God had just convicted me of closing my spirit. I repented for being angry and asked her to forgive me and to please feel free to correct me whenever I began to show any signs of doing the same thing again. I recognized that this attitude was so deeply ingrained in my spirit that I would need ongoing help to get out of, what had become for me, a rut.

I later recognized this trait in our son Deryk, and felt that I needed to expose this sin of mine to my three children. Bringing it to the light gave us the opportunity to arrest this insidious enemy whenever it tried to gain a foothold in our home.

Without my realizing it, Noline had been a victim of my hardening my heart against her for years. I had always blamed her and believed I had good reason for my deep-seated feelings, but I was wrong, and what I did wasn't helping to resolve anything. It only made matters worse.

Each time I did this, I lowered Noline's confidence level, making her more unsure of herself. God hated that because it prevented her from growing in Christ, as He desired. She often felt she had to walk on egg shells, just to keep me from being angry and withdrawn. And she would make an effort to prepare my favorite meal, just to win my approval.

In the case of being late, she had been wrong. But what I did was worse. She has since begun working on her part of the change. But I was the real problem, and God

Avoiding A Breakdown Of Communications

wanted to change me. As the head of our household, if I change first, the others change too. And sure enough, the minute I changed, Noline began to make a greater effort to be on time.

Today, Noline is a gifted speaker in her own right, communicating many helpful truths to the Body of Christ at large.

It is not always easy or convenient to use ourselves as examples, but I know that all married couples experience some of the same things. The closing of one's spirit is not restricted to men. Women also close their spirits to their husbands. I hope our example will encourage you to avoid the breakdown of communications that can be a death knell to any marriage. Instead, apply God's principles to your marriage so that you can experience a breaking loose and be able to take your marriage to a higher level of fulfillment.

CHAPTER NINE

UNDERSTANDING YOUR ENEMY — AND THE SPIRIT OF CONTROL

For our struggle is not against flesh and blood, but against the rulers, against the authorities, against the powers of this dark world and against the spiritual forces of evil in the heavenly realms.

Ephesians 6:12

We are not fighting against *"flesh and blood,"* and since my wife is *"flesh and blood,"* I know that she is not my real enemy. The devil would like us to concentrate on each other's weaknesses and the wrongs we have done to each other, and forget that our real battle is with him. Even though you cannot see him, he is always there, harassing and intimidating the saints of God, looking for ways to destroy them and claim victory. Satan is the Accuser of the Brethren, and it is time to expose the real enemy and his tactics, so that we can be properly focus on the problems we face.

There is nothing that pleases the devil more than our battling each other. Just as God hates divorce, Satan delights in it. He sees every divorce among believers as a slap in the face of the Savior. He believes that divorce among believers declares him the winner, for he has suc-

ceeded in splitting up another couple. He sees it as a failure of God, for the Almighty could not keep the two
together.

Of course, this is not a true picture. In reality it is the
couple who fails to turn to the Lord in their time of dis-
tress and to call upon Him. If we turn to Him, He can
intervene in our affairs. When we shut Him out, He is
powerless to help us. If we get so preoccupied with fighting each other and blaming each other, we may fail to
recognize the real enemy of our souls. Many do just that.

From the time he was in Heaven, as Lucifer, Satan has
wanted to rule, to have dominion. Blinded because of his
own beauty, he literally believed he could take over the
throne of the One who created him. He was driven by the
deep-seated sin of pride, manifested by his desire to control. Not satisfied with his exalted role, he wanted more
and more. He wanted to do things his own way. Convinc-
ing one third of the angels to follow him, he rebelled
against the Most High God.

The Bible shows us the result of such folly. Lucifer was
cast out of Heaven and was stripped of his heavenly authority. He now subverts the people of the earth, in a bid
to keep them in the kingdom of darkness, under his control.

It didn't take Satan long to decide that the way he
could hurt God the most was to hurt man, God's favorite
creation. If he could control the heart of man and turn
him from God, he would win. Man, after all, was created
in the image of God and had the nature of his Maker. The
temptation devised by Satan for Adam and Eve was not

only to change their allegiance from God to Satan himself, but to place them under Satan's direct control.

The tool that Satan used against man was to contradict God in His declaration that the couple would die if they ate the fruit of the Tree of the Knowledge of Good and Evil. They would not die, he assured Eve. Rather, something wonderful would happen. Their eyes would be opened, and they would be *like God.* God, of course, didn't want that to happen, Satan said, because God did not want you to know that you are like Him and could have control. That was the only reason He had told Adam and Eve not to eat the forbidden fruit. What other explanation could there be?

The thing Satan neglected to say was that Adam and Eve were already made in the image of God, they were under the special care and nurture of God, and their life was total bliss. They had no difficult decisions to make, for everything they could possibly need was provided for them. They could just enjoy God's provision and their fellowship with Him, for they lacked nothing.

Satan's astute plan was to plant a seed of discontent in the hearts of Adam and Eve, making them feel that they had no control over their own lives, that God was keeping something important and wonderful from them, something that He didn't want to share with them. And it worked!

The same desire for control that had caused Lucifer's exit from Heaven took hold of the hearts of Adam and Eve. They willingly chose to disobey God, accepting the lie that they would somehow gain new freedom by making their own choices and by having total control over their own future. They might even become *like God.*

Breaking Loose

Both Adam and Eve ate of the forbidden fruit, their eyes were opened, and they suddenly understood the difference between good and evil, between God and Satan; but it was too late. They were now under the control of their true enemy. He had deceived them. Banned from the Garden for their disobedience, and with death now at work in their lives, Adam and Even were helpless to control their own destiny.

They didn't lose everything. They were still free agents, still able to make choices, but they suddenly found themselves under Satan's thumb and subject to the fruits of disobedience.

Paul taught the Romans:

> *Don't you know that when you offer yourselves to someone to obey him as slaves, you are slaves to the one whom you obey — whether you are slaves to sin, which leads to death, or to obedience, which leads to righteousness?*   Romans 6:16

The devil had won Round #1 and had gained control over man, the most important part of God's creation.

When man made this fatal choice and yielded to the lies of Satan, he opened himself up to the devil's control and, in many ways, began to be like his adversary. The controlling spirit that had caused Satan's fall from grace now took hold of the heart of man.

Strangely enough, this philosophy of wanting to control one's own future seems to be the engine driving the flood of humanistic teaching so prominently accepted by our present generation. And so, because man insists on controlling his own future, he loses the very best that God has to offer him. The more control a man exercises over his own life, the less control God has. Therefore, Satan can have a field day with that life.

Like their master, fallen men and women seem to be constantly battling over control of their own lives and the lives of their mates. This drive to control, this controlling spirit, I believe, is the tap root to ninety percent of the family dysfunction experienced in our society.

Even children begin at a very early age trying to gain control over their parents. Our oldest daughter went through a period when she was only a few months old that was very trying. We would place her in her crib for the night, and immediately she would start crying. We would pick her up and hold her, and she would quiet down, stop her crying immediately, and even start gurgling and cooing. But the minute we put her back into the crib, she would start crying again.

At first, this was cute and we gave in to it, but not for long. We soon realized that if we continued to tolerate this behavior, we weren't going to get enough sleep ourselves. She wanted to be held for hours in the middle of the night after her feeding. So, if she didn't learn to go to sleep on her own after her feeding, or to lie in her crib and amuse herself, we weren't going to get enough rest in the coming weeks and months.

When she found that we did not cater to her every whim, she soon started sleeping normally.

Unsaved or natural men are chauvinistic and must try to take control over "their" woman — spiritually, emotionally and physically. Outside of Christ, a man is so insecure that he feels he must control others, and this is the single most devastating force of self-destruction in every marriage. The man desperately tries to maintain control, and if he feels threatened in this regard, he is overwhelmed by a deep sense of failure and reacts irrationally. One way he does this is to close his spirit. Another is to express anger through violence. And, in the worst cases, this desire for control can lead to murder or suicide, and even both at once.

In a woman, the tendency to want to control everything is no different, but it may manifest itself differently. The feminist movement was empowered by women who suffered under the domination of male chauvinists and were pushed down and treated like second-class citizens, like slaves in their own home. In a natural sense, they had a right to revolt. God didn't make women to be second-class citizens; He made them coequal with man.

Women revolted when the opportunity arose, and the unfortunate manifestation is radical feminism — the women's way of gaining control of their lives — and of everything and everyone else, for that matter.

Other women try to exert control through overeating, through starving themselves, or through emotionally controlling their husbands.

Each of us could make a long list of ways we have seen both men and women trying to control their marriage and their family life. This ongoing power struggle is the result of the fall of man in the Garden of Eden and man's subjection to Satan's control.

Just as Adam and Eve missed the point in the Garden, we today are missing the simplicity of the truth God

wants us to know. If you want to have a happy and meaningful life, the key is not how you can control your own
life and the lives of others, but how you can yield your
life to the control of God through Jesus Christ and
through the power of His Holy Spirit. Jesus said:

> *For whoever wants to save his life will lose it, but*
> *whoever loses his life for me will find it.*
>
> Matthew 16:25

He is our example, and He didn't seek control:

> *Jesus knew that the Father had put all things under*
> *his power, and that he had come from God and was*
> *returning to God; so he got up from the meal, took off*
> *his outer clothing, and wrapped a towel around his*
> *waist. After that, he poured water into a basin and*
> *began to wash his disciples' feet, drying them with*
> *the towel that was wrapped around him. He came to*
> *Simon Peter, who said to him, "Lord, are you going*
> *to wash my feet?" Jesus replied, "You do not realize*
> *now what I am doing, but later you will under-*
> *stand."*
> John 13:3-7

Jesus was attending the Feast of the Passover, just
hours before He would face the cross. This could have
been the most important dinner He ever had with His
disciples, and He wanted to show them *"the full extent of
His love."* (Verse 1) There was *"no greater love"* than His,
and He wanted them to understand that love. He would
now demonstrate it to them in several meaningful ways.

113

He told them that *"the Father had put all things under his power."* Jesus, then, had become the most powerful man that ever walked the face of the earth. Imagine having such power and authority placed in your hands! It is hard to grasp. If anyone could have exercised control, Jesus could have done it. He was a man of purpose and knew where He had come from and where He was going. He was a man of vision and direction, and God was with Him. He could call ten thousand angels to His side at any given moment.

And what did Jesus do with all the power entrusted to Him? Did He flaunt it, as many of us would have done? Did He flex His muscles, proving to everyone Who He was and what He could do? Did He demand a throne and call everyone to bow before Him and do His bidding?

Jesus could have done virtually anything He wanted, but, instead, He chose to take off His robe, His garment of authority, and to adorn Himself as a servant, with a towel about His waist. Then He did one of the most remarkable things of His entire ministry. He took a basin of water and began to wash the feet of His disciples. Was this the King of kings and the Lord of lords?

Our problem with understanding Christ in this context is that His Kingdom is altogether different from what we are used to, and its laws are entirely foreign to those of us who are steeped in this world's ways. "If you want to get true control over your life, give it up," He was saying to us. "If you seem to lose your life, that is when you actually gain it."

Jesus was even willing to give His life for others. He said:

Understanding Your Enemy

I tell you the truth, unless a kernel of wheat falls to the ground and dies, it remains only a single seed. But if it dies, it produces many seeds. The man who loves his life will lose it, while the man who hates his life in this world will keep it for eternal life.

John 12:24-25

Jesus chose not to use the power bestowed on Him for the purpose of controlling others, but rather to serve them. And what He did that day in Jerusalem was done as an example for all of us. We should do the same. This doesn't mean only that we wash one another's feet. It means that we humbly serve each other from the heart.

This is especially true in marriage. To insist that everything that is done be done "my" way and to please "me" robs me of God's best for my life. I can have His highest by being more concerned about the feelings and needs of my mate and how I can bless her. This defeats the spirit of control that Satan attempts to place upon each of us.

Paul wrote to the Philippian believers:

Therefore God exalted him to the highest place and gave him the name that is above every name, that at the name of Jesus every knee should bow, in heaven and on earth and under the earth, and every tongue confess that Jesus Christ is Lord, to the glory of God the Father. Therefore, my dear friends, as you have always obeyed — not only in my presence, but now much more in my absence — continue to work out your salvation with fear and trembling, for it is God

115

> *who works in you to will and to act according to his*
> *good purpose.*   Philippians 2:1-13

Jesus was equal with God the Father, yet He chose to lay down His superior position to demonstrate to us what life in His Kingdom is all about. If we would take on the mind of Christ and decide to be servants rather than overlords, God would bless us more, just as He blessed the life and ministry of His Son.

Not all of the disciples learned the lesson Jesus sought to give them through the foot-washing episode, for soon afterward a power struggle erupted among those close followers:

> *Also a dispute arose among them as to which of them*
> *was considered to be greatest.*   Luke 22:24

What did it matter, *"who was considered to be greatest"*? Why did they want to know, if not to seek to control one another? These men were all called to greatness and had absolutely no reason to be competing among themselves. They were to complement each other, not compete with each other.

This is true in the marriage setting. Since the husband and wife are one unit, and they are blessed or not blessed as a unit, why should one individual or the other always try to gain the upper hand? This type of competition serves no useful purpose. The husband is the husband, and the wife is the wife, and they are for each other.

We need to get rid of our worldly thinking, our carnal

mentality, and stop trying to compete with one another. God has called us rather to serve each other.

Marriage is not a competition. We are in this thing together. You are part of a team. Work for the good of the whole. This is the only way you can win. Either we win together, or we lose together. You decide.

Jesus showed His disciples that His methods are not to be confused with the ways of this world:

> *Jesus said to them, "The kings of the Gentiles lord it over them; and those who exercise authority over them call themselves Benefactors."*   Luke 22:25

The people of this world love control, so they lord it over each other at every opportunity. If we live the same way they do, we have not yet learned the principles of God's Kingdom. This phrase *"lord it over"* insinuates superiority, making oneself out as being superior, and another, as being inferior. This is clearly not God's way, and Jesus warned us against this kind of thinking. The constant struggle to see who will wear the pants in the family does not please Him.

People who lord it over others rule over them. This is clearly what the disciples had in mind when they asked who was greatest. In relating this to the marriage, much has been made in recent years of the teaching on headship and submission, with the greater emphasis on the fact that the husband should always be in control. After all, is he not the king and priest of his home? But Jesus showed us that even though the husband is the head of the home, he must not lord it over the other members of his family, as carnal men and women do. The husband, rather, is servant of both his wife and his children. This knowledge breaks the power of Satan and his controlling spirit in your life.

For the first twelve years of our marriage, I was guilty of living as the king in my own home, expecting my wife to wait on me hand and foot. Oddly enough, my fellow Christians supported me in this lifestyle, as it seemed right to us all: the husband in control, and the wife in submission to him. For those men who are selfish, and for those who have not yet understood the teachings of God's Kingdom, it *would* seem right. But if we want to be blessed of God, it is time to break with the traditions of men and to give the proper honor to our wives. They are not our slaves.

We never found any written law that allowed us to lord it over our wives, but it certainly was understood as being proper. I was the lord of my household, and I needed to be served. Since then, I have repented of that attitude and asked God to forgive me for my arrogance. I have asked my wife to forgive me, as well; for I was sinning against her when I allowed this worldly attitude to dominate my thinking.

One of the things that shocked me into reality was to see our son, the youngest of our three children, expecting his two older sisters to wait on him. When I noticed it, the Lord showed me that I was the one who influenced him to treat his sisters in such an arrogant manner. As a result, I repented before the whole family for being insensitive to the requirements of true leadership.

My recognition of God's truth, that we are all equal in

Understanding Your Enemy

His sight, and that none is to lord it over the other, has not made me any less of a man. If Jesus could be the most powerful man on earth and could refuse to exercise control over others, I can do the same. And my manhood is only enhanced by the experience.

I am head of my wife, just as Jesus is the Head of the Church. And since He gave Himself for the Church, I must give myself for my wife. Headship does not mean that I have the right to lord it over everyone else.

God is a God of order, and He works through direct lines of authority. That does not mean, however, that He sets me up in my private dictatorship. Order does not mean control or lording it over others.

That phrase *"lord it over"* also means "taking dominion." Because I was the extrovert in our family, it was easy for me to dominate our relationship from the very beginning. But just because Noline is quiet and reflective does not mean that she is weak. On the contrary, she is the more stable of the two. With my personality, I tend to have mood swings, depending on the circumstances, while Noline is more even-tempered and balanced, not easily swayed by present circumstances. So, in every situation, extroverts need to demonstrate self-control, one of the fruits of the Spirit, and not people-control.

None of us like it when a domineering person suddenly and rudely barges in on a private conversation and takes it over. And we must not be guilty of that either. This is the way of the world. Pastors and other church leaders, husbands and businessmen alike, all need to heed this teaching of Jesus.

Women are just as guilty as men. There are many

strong personalities among woman, and that is a God-given gift, but not so that they can dominate relationships.

The phrase *"lord it over"* also refers to "those who use influence to gain control." This may be a more subtle form of controlling. One of the strengths that God gave the man was the ability to conquer and to produce income. Men have historically held the reins of finance. This does not mean, however, that it is proper to use finances as a tool to control others, especially your own wife.

Most men want to hold the purse strings tightly. They give their wives a "housekeeping allowance," but they maintain control of all the major purchases, the house, the cars, the stocks and bonds, etc. If the man is more gifted in this area, this may be all well and good, but too often that is not the case, and the family suffers as a result. Too many men feel that if they give their wives control over the family finances, their own image suffers.

The day we get married, it is no longer "my money," it is "our money." No matter who earns it, it belongs to both of us, and both of us should share in the decisions about how it is spent or how it is invested.

I have been guilty of dangling before my wife the possibility of buying her something if she came around to my way of thinking on some matter. This is financial tyranny.

Woman have other tools that they sometimes misuse for control. One of them is sex. God has blessed the woman with the power of sexual intimacy, and women have been known to use that power to gain favor with men. Married women often use sex as a weapon against their husbands, withholding their favors when things don't go their way.

The Bible speaks very clearly to this problem, showing us that our bodies are not our own. We belong to each other and were given for each others' pleasure. Christian women cannot expect to act like women of the world and be blessed of God in their relationships.

"If you will go shopping with me, and let me buy that new dress I have been wanting, I'll show you a good time tonight." This is not a Christian approach to a relationship, but an example of using our strengths to lord it over others. Christian women should be different.

This phrase *"lord it over"* again implies "the use of raw brute force in order to control the lives of others". Earthly kings will sometimes stop at nothing to get what they want. They have been known to place innocent men and women into slavery to accomplish their desired goals. Killing, maiming, torture and physical dominance — a worldly leader seeking to rise to the top and to keep others under his control is not above any of these things.

In the marriage, some men are too quick to use violence in their relationship so that they can dominate, and God hates that. He made men bigger and stronger for a reason, and it wasn't so that they could beat on their wives. As Malachi declared:

> *"I hate divorce," says the LORD God of Israel, "and I hate a man's covering himself with violence as well as with his garment," says the LORD Almighty. So guard yourself in your spirit, and do not break faith.*
> Malachi 2:16

God hates this type of abuse. It is everything He is not. God is love, and operates out of love. Love is not weak, when it is properly directed. Brute strength just won't get the job done. For more on the special action needed in cases of abuse, see chapter eleven, "Doing the Right Thing In Cases of Abuse."

The next thing Jesus said to His disciples that day was that the people of the world *exercise authority* over others. This phrase means "to use and have total power over another at your will and choosing; to be an authority figure." In every family, disputes arise about who is in charge. Who will make decisions concerning the children? Who will make decisions concerning the family finances? Who will make decisions about the frequency of sexual intimacy in the relationship? And we have all learned techniques to get our own way.

When I want to do something or I want to buy something, I make myself an authority on the subject, so that Noline doesn't know how to argue with me on the matter, and I can do what I want to do. This sometimes has disastrous results.

Once I desperately wanted to buy a certain automobile. When I took Noline to see the car, however, she sat in it for a minute and immediately declared that she didn't like it because it "smelled funny." I explained to her that what she was smelling was diesel fuel, and that this is what set the car apart from all others. "You can drive this car through a swollen river," I told her, "and the motor won't cut out on you like a gasoline engine with spark plugs will. Once you have started the car, you could even take the battery out, and it will still run." I'm not sure why I thought that was important, but it sounded good. In the end, I convinced Noline, and we bought the car. But was it the right thing to do?

Before three months had passed the diesel pump went out on that car, and it proved a very costly part to replace. Then other things began to go wrong. In the end, so many things went wrong that we ended up giving the car away. I won that particular battle through the use of my knowledge on the subject, but our family lost financially in the end.

The earthly leaders about whom Jesus spoke saw themselves as worthy *"benefactors"* of the adulation and service of those around them. Because of their years of faithful service, they considered that this was the least others could do for them. There was no sense of their responsibility to others, but only of others to them. They were quick to let everyone know how great they were and how dependent others were on them for everything.

Husbands often use these tactics. As the one who brings in the paycheck, who provides the "bread and butter" for the household, they consider themselves worthy of special honor. Although this has greatly changed in today's world, and there are more two-income families, the problem of men trying to control everything through their position as breadwinner of the family is still a serious one and must be dealt with.

In many other ways, we all try to throw our weight around, hoping to receive special honor. But this is a battle you just can't win. The battlefield is strewn with the bodies of those who tried.

Once Noline and I were teaching on this subject at a

marriage retreat. To demonstrate to the audience the fact that I, as the head of the family, and the physically stronger of the two, needed to take my position humbly at my wife's feet and show her honor, I acted it out. I took off my jacket, showing that I was determined to rid myself of the old chauvinistic lifestyle and to put on the new life patterned after Christ. Then, I took that jacket and tied it around my waist like a towel. I got down on my knees before my wife, removed her shoes, and started to reenact the washing of her feet. All the while, I was looking up into her face and affirming to her my love, and my commitment to loyalty and faithfulness.

After a little while, the whole crowd erupted in applause and whistles, as everyone stood to their feet in appreciation. I can assure you that their response was not elicited by my acting ability. It was because people were seeing something that struck a chord, something they wanted in their own lives.

The men were cheering, as well as the women. Both of them wanted, more than anything else, to break loose from the pattern of failure in their married lives and to try something that worked for a change. People everywhere hate phoniness and long for real experiences that can change our everyday lives. After we have attended hundreds or even thousands of church services and listened to hundreds or even thousands of great speakers, it doesn't count for very much if we can't take it back home and live it.

We have to start somewhere. When I made my change in driving and moved to the other side of the road, there was a definite starting point. It was the first time I got behind the wheel in this county. But we can each find a definite place to start in demonstrating our new attitude.

One of my starting points in honoring my wife in the home was to start helping her more with the chores around the house. Noline had always come under great pressure when we were having guests over, and the house needed to be tidied up. Her whole demeanor changed when, one day, she found the kitchen unexpectedly cleaned up and the dishes all washed. That did more for her than if I had gone out and bought her a dozen roses. The roses would have been great, but the house would still have needed cleaning, and Noline would still have felt frustrated. What she needed more than roses was a little help around the house.

Rather than worry about who is in control, I must commit myself to making my strengths and abilities available to my wife for the purpose of building a home that is strong and to let her know that she can depend on me when she needs me. As a woman and wife, she must respond in like manner with her strengths and abilities, making her feelings and decisions available to me. Together, then, we can make the full transition into life in the Kingdom.

If we can understand the evils of the spirit of control and both guard against it, we will have taken a giant step toward breaking loose from the chains that hold us and taking our marriage to a higher level of fulfillment.

CHAPTER TEN

DEALING WITH ANGER

*Get rid of all bitterness, rage and anger, brawling
and slander, along with every form of malice. Be
kind and compassionate to one another, forgiving
each other, just as in Christ God forgave you.*

Ephesians 4:31-32

Anger and the violence it spawns is not just an inner-city or gang-related problem. The violence in our large cities gets most of the publicity, but the most volatile place on the face of the earth is not the dark streets of our major cities or the back alleys of some downtrodden community. It is the average home, for it is in the home that ninety percent of violent crimes against women occur. Much of this violence never makes the headlines, and a large portion of it is never reported to any authority.

Of all the sad statistics on violence that we have seen in recent years, the fact that really shook Noline and me was that *husbands* are the most common perpetrators of acts of violence against women in America. The very relationship that God devised for the most intense and rewarding experience of a woman's life, has turned violently and destructively against her. What a shame!

As we have seen, God hates divorce, and He hates the fact that men use violence as a tool to control their spouses. The phrase that God used in Malachi denotes that man uses his anger as a *"cloak"* or a *"covering."* It may not be seen on the surface, but push a few buttons, and it quickly comes to light.

Sometimes even Christian men demonstrate these traits. When they do, it means they desperately need to take off their cloak of worldly response, and put on the gentleness and meekness of Christ. Violence is part of the reaction of the past life and should play no part in the Christian marriage.

Noline and I do not claim to be experts on this subject, in the technical sense, but we do know what the Scriptures say on the subject and have testimony of what God has done, both in our own lives and in the lives of others with whom we are closely associated. We can learn to deal with anger in a Christian way.

Much is said in Scripture of *"envy"* and *"strife"*:

> For where envying and strife is, there is confusion
> and every evil work.   James 3:16 (KJV)

The word translated here as *envy* means "a feeling of discontent and ill-will because of another's advantage, and the desire to possess the same advantage." Envy starts with one spouse wanting to replace the other.

Why is it that we hate for our partners to "get the upper hand" in any argument? It's because we are envious. We want "the upper hand" ourselves.

Dealing With Anger

This word *strife* means "the act of striving, contention, quarrel, struggle." The conflicts that become the center of strife for any couple could be resolved in other ways, but strife often feeds on itself, and the debate grows ever more venomous until something ugly happens. Human nature is such that each of us wants to win every argument, regardless of the cost. That's why we often say and do things that we don't really mean, and for which we are later sorry.

At the moment, we can't realize the long-term damage a foolish word or a foolish act can have. All we can think about is winning the pending argument. Often we even expect our mates to quickly forget what we say in heated moments, since we really didn't mean it anyway. But, as we learn too late, it doesn't work that way. Instead, our foolish words become seeds that are sown and that will later take root and grow, bringing forth a sure and deadly harvest.

The word here translated *confusion* means "disorder, bewilderment, embarrassment, failure to distinguish between things." Saying things in the heat of argument that don't come from the heart and that are intended to gain momentary advantage opens the door to confusion in our relationship. It undermines the truths that we hold in our hearts, and we come to believe that the person to whom we have been joined is really our worst enemy in the world, and doesn't love us after all. This type of confusion further opens the door to *"every evil work."*

The word here translated *evil* means "morally bad or wrong, wicked, depraved." How could any man commit acts of violence against the people he loves? How could a man beat or maim or kill his own wife? Is he a beast of some kind? Is he sick or inhuman?

Probably no husband or wife wakes up one morning thinking to himself or herself, "Today, I'm going to kill my wife (or husband)." These acts of violence take place because of the envy and strife and confusion that are allowed to come into a relationship over a period of time. One thing leads to another and the pressure builds, until a person feels powerless to change things, powerless to turn things around, and so hurt by what has been said and what has been done that he or she reacts in a violent way.

Powerlessness brings about a sense of having lost all control and having no hope of being able to regain that control. When we feel that things have gone beyond the boundaries that we can handle, we get desperate and angry.

There are two important things to know about anger: (1) there is a right anger, and there is a wrong anger, and (2) there is a right way to express anger, and there is a wrong way to express anger. Some of us learned proper and improper anger from our parents when we were children. Others, however, are from homes where they had no proper role models. Since all parents are imperfect in some sense, many of us have a lot to learn in this regard.

The Scriptures teach us:

> *And, ye fathers, provoke not your children to wrath: but bring them up in the nurture and admonition of the Lord.* Ephesians 6:4 (KJV)

Dealing With Anger

Parents must employ a godly nurturing that teaches their children to cope with life's difficulties by calling on the strength of the Lord, and not through trusting their own brute strength.

Small children can show anger. When they don't get their way, they cry. If that doesn't work, they start screaming, and can follow that up with a tantrum, if need be. Once you pick them up, you have begun to teach them that if they scream loud enough, they will get what they want and avoid the nap or whatever it is they are protesting. If left unchecked, a child with such tendencies will soon turn into a tyrant, always demanding his way, whether what he wants is convenient to his parents or not. We need to start early showing our children that we don't reward wrong anger, and we must not reward temper tantrums.

If children have their way when they are young, by their teenage years temper tantrums may change to disrespectful verbal responses to parents and teenagers getting their own way. This is very dangerous, and parents who allow it to happen often suffer emotionally because they blame themselves for their children's resultant failures.

Many of the failures we suffer with our teenagers indicates a failure to deal with the growing child in the crib. A little discipline goes a long way, and simply allowing a child to cry itself to sleep rather than have its own way every time is good training that will pay off in years to come.

When a child is wet or hungry or not feeling well, that is one thing, but selfishness and disobedience and outburst of uncontrolled anger must not be tolerated. When children grow up having their own way in everything, they often take that attitude into the marriage relationship. If they are not able to die to self and to come to Christ and be delivered from the attitudes that have dominated their childhood, they will go on acting like spoiled brats and will ultimately destroy the marriage.

We had some problems with Deryk when he was a teenager, and once he was even suspended from school for two weeks. We were doing a lot of traveling for the ministry in those days, and his problems put a lot of strain on us — and on him.

Just after his expulsion, Noline and I were on one of our trips and had to drive from Pennsylvania to Connecticut, some eight hours on the road. While we were driving along, we got into a heated discussion about what was happening in our son's life. We hashed everything out, backward and forward, over and over again.

What part of Deryk's failure was our own fault? What had caused him to act in this way? Had the School Board been fair in its decision? And on and on and on it went. By the time we reached our destination, I was exhausted, mostly from driving so long, but also from discussing this problem ad infinitum.

We stayed with a couple in their very luxurious home, and they put us in their beautiful master bedroom. I was so tired that when my head hit the pillow, I fell asleep immediately. No sooner had I drifted off to sleep, however, than I felt myself being pulled back into consciousness by Noline. She still couldn't stop talking about

Dealing With Anger

Deryk and his problems. "Honey," I pleaded, "I really need to get some rest," and I drifted back to sleep.

But she couldn't let it rest, and once again woke me by insisting on continuing our discussion of the matter.

When this happened a third time, I opened my eyes, turned to Noline and said very sternly, "Go to sleep." But Noline was so upset by what we had been discussing that my seeming insensitivity to her feelings set off something inside her. She jumped up and, standing on the bed, ripped the blankets off, threw them on the floor and then made a bed for herself there. "You are the most insensitive person I have ever come across," she said in a hushed, angry tone, as she settled down in her new bed.

This type of anger is not uncommon. It is manifested when a person is seemingly tolerant of a situation for a great length of time, but underneath, because there has been no resolution, something is boiling. At some moment, that anger is going to spew forth.

Noline felt totally powerlessness over the expulsion of our son and was humiliated by the scandal it caused in our community. The problem had been boiling under the surface for a while and my being tired seemed to say to her that I wasn't sufficiently interested in what she was feeling, so she exploded in the Connecticut night. What should I do now?

I lay there for a few minutes, with just a sheet left covering me. I was so tired, I almost didn't care. I thought of just leaving Noline where she was. Maybe we could both get some sleep. The fact that we are involved in marriage ministries, however, and were actively trying to help other people deal with their marriage conflicts, just wouldn't let me do that. If we don't practice what we preach, how can we continue to make recommendations to others?

"Let's take a strife break," I said. A "strife break" is a tool we learned from the Married For Life course, a tool that helps couples deal with the anger they experience. Both parties agree to pray in the Spirit for three minutes. A three-minute prayer doesn't necessarily resolve the issue that has caused the strife, but it gives everyone a chance to cool off and to get out of the flesh and into the Spirit so that they can deal with the situation at hand in a proper and levelheaded way. Then, when we face things, it is not from a sense of powerlessness, but from a sense of the assurance that the power of God is with us.

Thank God we were able to calm down that night and to sleep, knowing that we both cared about the situation and were both determined to do all that we could to resolve our son's difficulties.

None of us is exempt from outbursts of anger, and anger, in itself, is not necessarily wrong. It is the continual use of this strong emotion to gain control over someone else and to insist on having our own way that is wrong.

I have had my own lapses. When Deryk turned sixteen, he begged us to let him have our '86 Buick Century and to buy a new car for ourselves. We had purchased the Buick new and had taken good care of it, so that, although it had more than 120,000 miles on it, it still wasn't using any oil. We prayed about this proposal and eventually decided that it would be good for him to use the older car as his first automobile. I did, however, place some conditions on his driving. He had to make sure that the oil was changed regularly and that the car was kept clean. He was to wear his safety belt at all times and was not to drive faster than the posted speed limits.

Several months went by, and it seemed that Deryk was keeping his end of the bargain. One day I noticed that he was parking the car under a tree, away from the house or alongside the garage where nobody walked, and this seemed a little strange, but I didn't give it a second thought. Then one morning, as he was backing the car out, on his way to school, I was standing at the kitchen window, washing some coffee mugs, when I suddenly caught a glimpse of the front of the car. My beautiful old Buick seemed to have the front end smashed in.

I couldn't believe what I was seeing and ran from the kitchen through to the living room to get another look, as he passed by there. Sure enough, the car had been damaged somehow.

All day, while our son was at school, the knowledge of what he had done boiled higher and higher inside of me. The fact that he had somehow smashed in the front of that perfectly-kept old car was bad enough, but the fact that he was trying to hide those facts from us was much worse. How could he do such a thing? "He's going to get it when he gets home," I told Noline. She tried to calm me, but I refused to be consoled. This was a serious matter that required serious action.

The minute the boy came in the door, I was in his face, letting him know just how angry I was. I let him know how disappointed I was in his rotten driving, in the fact that he had been so careless as to do a thing like that, and, more so, that he had tried to hide the facts from us. Not only had he wrecked the car, but he had been deceptive. And he should know better, since he was a Christian.

At this point, I grabbed his shirt and pulled him out the back door and toward the car, yelling all the while about what a terrible thing he had done. When I got to the car, I was so upset that I kicked it. "Do you want to see how to wreck a car?" I asked. "I'll show you how to wreck a car." With that, I grabbed the antenna and ripped it from the car, snapping it in two before his eyes. "If you want to wreck a car, it's not hard to do," I insisted. "See how easy that was?" By this time he was in tears, and I was satisfied that I had said enough and that he had learned his lesson.

Two days later we were on our way toward Michigan to teach at a marriage seminar, and as we were driving up the interstate, the Spirit of God began to convict my heart. That morning, in my devotions, I had been reading from Isaiah:

> *See my servant, whom I uphold; my Chosen One, in whom I delight. I have put my Spirit upon him; he will reveal justice to the nations of the world. He will be gentle. He will not shout nor quarrel in the streets. He will not break the bruised reed, nor quench the dimly burning flame. He will encourage the fainthearted, those who are tempted to despair. He will see full justice given to all who have been wronged. He won't be satisfied until truth and righteousness prevail throughout the earth, nor until even distant lands beyond the seas have put their trust in him.* Isaiah 42:1-4 (TLB)

Dealing With Anger

I knew that I was God's servant too, and the Spirit was reminding me that I needed to be gentle, like Jesus. I saw that He had not shouted in the streets. In my case, it was the driveway. He did not *"break the bruised reed,"* and that was the point that had really gotten to me — for I had broken the antenna. I should have been a man of encouragement, as Jesus was. What I did to my son was not helpful.

I repented right there in my wife's presence and asked both her and the Lord to forgive me. After we had talked for a while about it, Noline said that she felt it would mean a lot to our son if I called him and asked his forgiveness too. The next time we stopped for gas, I found a phone and called home. When I told my son how wrong I had been and how sorry I was and asked him to forgive me, he told me that he had reacted very negatively to my anger. "If this is how my father behaves, and he is a Christian, then I don't want to be a Christian any longer," he had said to himself. I am sure that my willingness to recognize my wrong and ask his forgiveness that day saved our relationship as father and son from a more serious deterioration. And it also seemed to save the relationship between my son and his heavenly Father.

The Scriptures teach the right way to handle our anger:

> *Be ye angry, and sin not: Let not the sun go down upon your wrath.*   Ephesians 4:26 (KJV)

God has placed within every one of us a strong passion against injustice, and we feel angry when we see things

137

that are wrong. Jesus Himself felt this when He saw the Temple polluted, made into *"a den of thieves."* But there is a proper way to react. Even healthy anger must be properly channelled.

When we see people do wrong things, the first thing we must consider is that Satan is behind the wrong act, and we must pray and bind his power. We must take the authority available to us, through the name of Jesus, and use it positively. We must resist him, as James taught:

> *Submit yourselves, then, to God. Resist the devil, and he will flee from you.* James 4:7

Don't take the emotions that have been aroused because of evil and use them against people. People are not our enemies. Satan is.

As a very good example, when a baby uses a tantrum to get its own way, that is clearly wrong. But it is much more wrong for a parent to storm into the child's bedroom and start shaking the child violently.

If I had hit Noline because I was tired and wanted to get some sleep, perhaps some would have found a way to justify that action, but it is clearly not God's way of dealing with a situation. My taking her by the hand and joining her in prayer brought a proper solution to the matter.

God's Word declares:

> *Man's anger does not bring about the righteous life that God desires.* James 1:20

Dealing With Anger

Using anger wrongly is a sin against God and against others.

When we respond correctly to feelings of anger, we can convey openly, honestly, and truthfully what we are feeling and sensing about the situation that has aroused our emotions, and we can do it in a logical way. There are ways of dealing with injustice, and this is the way that brings rewards.

One good example is the well-known organization MADD, which stands for Mothers Against Drunk Driving. This entire organization is made up of women who have lost children due to the negligence of drunken drivers. These women could take their anger out in other ways against the people who senselessly took from them a loved one, but they have chosen to respond in a positive way. They teach teenagers in local high schools about the damaging effects of drinking and driving, and they attempt to positively influence legislation on a local, state, and national level to stiffen the penalties against drunken driving. Everyone agrees that this is a wonderful attitude to have.

I believe those women are angry and have every right to be, but I respect them for channelling their anger into something positive.

Some people have told me that, in all the years of their married life, they have never experienced anger. I have to wonder about those people. Are they living in a dream world, where they are never attacked by the devil? Or have they learned to avoid any emotion? While their statement sounds great, it seems to ring false to me.

How can we not be angry at some of the things that are

happening in our world? Yet we must react positively, not negatively. People who are angry by the senseless death of so many aborted babies have a choice. They can either picket peacefully outside some abortion clinic, or they can start killing doctors who perform abortions. I think we all know which reaction is the correct one.

Anger is a normal and God-given reaction to injustice, so don't try to stifle it. Just learn to deal with it and to channel it correctly.

It is sometimes difficult to learn to deal with anger in a relationship if we have gotten in the habit of using our anger in an ungodly manner. Here are some steps that I have found helpful:

The first step in dealing with anger is to get yourself right spiritually. If there is any known sin in your life that is opening the door to a sense of failure and ultimate powerlessness, you need to repent of that sin before the Lord and ask His forgiveness.

You need to feed your spiritual life with the Word on a daily basis. This must be followed by prayer, so that you give God a chance to speak to your heart in areas where you may be out of fellowship with Him. You may also need to confess to your spouse areas of failure and compromise, as these may be leading you to a sense of hopelessness or powerlessness, and then into ungodly control.

The second helpful step in dealing with anger is to check your emotional life. You may be emotionally drained because of the existing circumstances of your job or home life or because of something that is happening at your church. You may need to take time to rebuild yourself in areas of emotional burnout.

Take time to read quality books that can feed your heart and mind. Noline and I set a goal one year to read a book each month.

Do something that you enjoy as a hobby, so that you can relax and have a change of pace once in a while. Noline likes crafts, so she took time each week that year to do some crafts. Most people nowadays "relax" by watching television, but most television programming is not relaxing and often has other negative effects.

Take some time just to reflect and be introspective so you can be in touch with your feelings.

Another important step may be to take better care of yourself physically. You may be out of shape and need to get more exercise, tone up, and eat the right foods, so that you can allow your body to be pleasing to God and to your mate. Being out of shape often leads to discouragement and to anger. Have regular physical checkups because many people are discovering chemical imbalances that affect their disposition. Some may even have more serious emotional disorders that can be discovered with regular checkups and successfully treated.

When you get upset, try to take note of what upset you. Many people don't even know what they are upset about. The documentation of a day's events may lead you to a diagnosis of your problem and be a first step toward your healing.

Pray with your spouse and, if need be, with other Christian leaders about the things that keep you from victory. Sometimes it helps to get a third person involved.

Whatever it takes, you must conquer anger. Shake off the cloak of violence that God hates. Be renewed in the spirit of your minds as you develop your life in God's Kingdom. In doing this, you will begin to break loose from your past patterns of behavior to take your marriage to a higher level of fulfillment.

CHAPTER ELEVEN

DOING THE RIGHT THING
IN CASES OF ABUSE

To the married I give this command (not I, but the Lord): A wife must not separate from her husband. But if she does, she must remain unmarried or else be reconciled to her husband. And a husband must not divorce his wife. 1 Corinthians 7:11-12

The matter of physical and emotional abuse is a serious one that demands our special attention. We can say, however, that the Bible fully addresses this issue.

There are cases where a wife has every reason to separate from her husband. No woman should be forced to stay in the same house with a man who is physically or emotionally abusing her. Life is a precious gift from God and must be protected and preserved at all cost.

But that does not free women of abusive relationships to automatically divorce their mates and seek another. God gives the woman permission to separate from an impossible mate, but He then gives her two alternatives: *"remain unmarried"* or *"be reconciled to her husband."* In the present climate of permissiveness and self-seeking, this may seem harsh to many. So why did God tell the woman who simply cannot live with her husband to concentrate on reconciliation or else remain unmarried?

Let us try to look at this situation from God's perspective. He is a loving and gracious God who desires that all be saved, even the abusers. When He commands the abused wife to *"remain unmarried,"* it is so that she can stand in faith and prayer for the complete deliverance of her husband, not simply abandon him to the fates. God doesn't compel her to stay in an abusive situation, but He also doesn't free her to break her vows to the Almighty.

Who are we to stand in judgment of abusers? Have we forgotten that it took a miracle to get each of us saved? And has God run out of miracles? While it is true that it will take a miracle to bring a wayward and abusive husband to salvation, God is in the miracle working business, and nothing is too hard for Him.

We give up far too quickly on these cases. At the first sign of smoke, we are heading for the exits. But what happened to the power of the cross? What happened to faith and prayer and perseverance?

The heroes of faith, mentioned in Hebrews 11, were not those who gave up on every situation and ran away to hide. They were those who stood firm (in seemingly impossible situations) and believed God for victory:

> *And what more shall I say? I do not have time to tell about Gideon, Barak, Samson, Jephthah, David, Samuel and the prophets, who through faith conquered kingdoms, administered justice, and gained what was promised; who shut the mouths of lions, quenched the fury of the flames, and escaped the edge*

Doing the Right Thing In Cases of Abuse

of the sword; whose weakness was turned to strength; and who became powerful in battle and routed foreign armies. Women received back their dead, raised to life again. Others were tortured and refused to be released, so that they might gain a better resurrection. Some faced jeers and flogging, while still others were chained and put in prison. They were stoned; they were sawed in two; they were put to death by the sword. They went about in sheepskins and goatskins, destitute, persecuted and mistreated — the world was not worthy of them. They wandered in deserts and mountains, and in caves and holes in the ground. These were all commended for their faith, yet none of them received what had been promised. God had planned something better for us so that only together with us would they be made perfect.   Hebrews 11:32-40

And you thought you had problems! It almost takes your breath away to think of the situations these people faced, yet they all overcame through faith in God. Nothing is impossible to Him. The writer of the Hebrews ended this section by saying:

Therefore, since we are surrounded by such a great cloud of witnesses, let us throw off everything that hinders and the sin that so easily entangles, and let us run with perseverance the race marked out for us. Let us fix our eyes on Jesus, the author and perfecter of our faith.   Hebrews 12:1-2

These are the secrets of success in difficult situations: *"throw off everything that hinders," "run with perseverance the race marked out for us,"* and *"fix [your] eyes on Jesus."* Just as He is the *"author"* of marriage, He is the *"perfecter,"* as well. The King James Version says, *"the finisher."* He is able to finish what He has begun.

God has not changed. What has changed is that instead of looking to men and women of faith, we are looking to this world's experts to give us the answers we need in abusive situations. Fix your eyes on Him. He still knows how to make crooked places straight, how to make rough places smooth, and how to remove offending mountains. Believe Him for your situation.

Also we must consider what makes men into abusers. Usually, men do not just get up one morning and begin to beat on their spouse for no apparent reason. In cases of alcoholism and drug abuse, the reason is apparent. But many men have deep-seated anger that has never been properly dealt with and it builds up in them until they explode. That doesn't make it any easier to bear, but at least we can understand where it comes from and what causes it and can appreciate the fact that any one of us might be an abuser if it were not for the grace of God in our lives.

A homicide detective shared with us that before he knew Christ he had the habit of threatening his Christian wife with his service revolver. When things weren't going his way, he would whip out that revolver and either threaten to kill her or threaten to kill himself, and he was serious. Maybe that shouldn't surprise us. After all, he was a man of the world, using the methods of the world, to keep and gain control through violent behavior. It is done every day, all over the world. The fact that this man was hired by a major American city to protect its citizens from violence is rather scary. He was doing exactly the same thing he was hired to prevent others from doing. In the end, his wife separated from him for fear for her life and because of all the hurts he had inflicted upon her. She was angry with God and was no longer willing to follow His plan for marriage.

During this separation the man found Christ and was born-again. After he was saved, he immediately began to pray and believe God for his marriage. This woman was his wife, and he had made a vow to God to love her "till death us do part." Yes, he had been abusive, but he just needed to be saved — in the same way she had needed to be saved.

The healing didn't happen overnight. It took some time of faith and prayer and perseverance, but this man refused to give up on his wife, refused to abandon her to the forces of Satan, refused to do the easy thing, by divorcing her and marrying another. And his answer came. It always does to those who are persistent and determined. Through his prayers and faith, through daily making the right choices, and through getting victory over the spirit of control that had motivated him so strongly in the past, and that had proved to be the root of their marital conflicts, his life gradually took on a new direction.

He later testified that even after he had been set free from demonic influences, he had to change his thinking and train himself not to react in the same violent manner he had before. Eventually he was able to successfully make the transition, from the violence of the kingdom of this world, to the gentleness and kindness of the Kingdom of God. He and his wife were reunited, and today they are being greatly used by the Lord in a ministry to other couples in difficult circumstances.

Temporary separation in cases of abuse serves a useful purpose. It provides safety for the abused party and allows that person, usually the wife, to stand in faith for her abusive mate. Therefore, if any abusing husband refuses to change, refuses to get counsel or professional help, the wife is under no obligation to remain under his control at home, for that could, at any time, become life threatening.

That is not the hard part. Most everyone agrees on that part. Most everyone recommends separation in these cases. The hard part comes when the world gives up on that abusing person, writes him off as "without hope of ever changing," and encourages the abused spouse to "get on with her life," divorcing the abuser and marrying another. This is clearly not God's perfect will.

If she abandons that man and turns from him completely, who will stand for his salvation? Who will bring him before the throne of God? Who will believe for him? Divorce and remarriage is not the first thing this woman should think about. It is something she should never think about. God wants reconciliation, and if that is impossible or takes time, he encourages her to *"remain unmarried."*

Every Christian has been given *"the ministry of reconciliation"*:

> *All this is from God, who reconciled us to himself*
> *through Christ and gave us the ministry of recon-*

Doing the Right Thing In Cases of Abuse

ciliation: that God was reconciling the world to himself in Christ, not counting men's sins against them. And he has committed to us the message of reconciliation.   2 Corinthians 5:18-19

Just as we were *"reconciled"* and just as our sins were *"not counted"* against us anymore, God wants us to actively pursue others who need reconciliation. That doesn't just mean the people of pagan religions in some other part of the world, or criminals in prison, or drug dealers on our streets. It means your husband or your wife.

We are not offering a simplistic answer for a complex problem here. The laws of many states actually require that abusive behavior be reported, and that state authorities get involved. We believe in extensive professional help for those who are abusive. Spiritually, however, we must believe God for their complete deliverance from the spirits of violence and anger, and we must help them learn how to control their bad temper. Whatever it takes to have the man free is what needs to happen, and we believe that the woman has a vital part to play in this healing and restoration process. If she is removed from the scene, the chances of her husband recovering are greatly reduced.

The world's solutions are the simplistic ones. You are married to a person with a problem, so leave them and find someone else who can make you happy. How sad that the church, rather than face these difficult situations and lend the support necessary to resolve them, often accepts the simplistic answers of carnal counselors as the best solution for everyone concerned. May God help us.

If a woman makes a vow before God that, "for better or for worse," she will stick by her man, how then is she justified in heading for the exit the minute the "worse" shows up? If it happens to you, believe God for a miracle. Believe His Word. Believe in the power of prayer. And believe in the convicting power of the Holy Spirit. Don't head for the exit. Stay and help put out the fire.

Exactly the same thing applies for a man whose wife is wayward and is having an adulterous affair. The husband is under command not to divorce her, because God's will is reconciliation. He wants that man to stand in faith, to believe God for the necessary miracle. After all, he made a vow before God that "for better or for worse," he would stick by this woman. How can he now be justified in the eyes of God if he is guilty of heading for the exit the minute the "worse" appears?

That man needs to pray for his wife, not divorce her. If she does not seem to respond at first, and even separates from him or begins divorce proceedings against him, he must continue to stand in faith for her, always remembering his vows. These are the moments that test our resolve. All of us can do well when everything goes our way, but few can stand when trouble comes. God is bigger than your spouse's waywardness, and your prayers may be the only true link to salvation for her soul.

Separation, when it is absolutely necessary, should be accomplished only for a divine purpose — reconciliation and redemption. This is God's best for the marriage. When we are willing to do things God's way, it enables us to break loose and to take our marriage to a higher level of fulfillment.

CHAPTER TWELVE

STARTING NOW TO COLONIZE YOUR WORLD FOR CHRIST

But when the fullness of time was come, God sent forth his son, made of a woman, made under the law.
Galatians 4:4 (KJV)

Go ye therefore, and teach all nations, baptizing them in the name of the Father, and of the Son, and of the Holy Ghost: Teaching them to observe all things whatsoever I have commanded you: and, lo, I am with you alway, even unto the end of the world. Amen.
Matthew 28:19-20

The coming of Jesus into the world was appointed by God for a set time. This word *"time"* is from the Greek word *chronos* which means "a completed period of time." God determined that after a certain period of time in the history of the world His Son Jesus would come on the scene. I personally believe that one of the reasons Jesus came when He did is related to the period in which He appeared, the period of the Roman Empire.

One of the dreams interpreted by the prophet Daniel foretold the rise and fall of five major world powers that would rule successively much of the known world before the end of time, as we know it. Nebuchadnezzar saw an image which he described in some detail.

The image had a head of gold, which represented the Babylonian Empire (606–538 BC). The chest and arms of the image were of silver and represented the Medeo/Persian Empire (538—331 BC). The belly and thighs of the image were of bronze and represented the Grecian Empire (331—168 BC). The legs of the image were of iron and represented the Roman Empire (168 BC to 100 AD). And the feet and toes of the image were a mixture of iron and clay and represent the time in which we now live. Jesus could have come in any one of those times, but the Father chose to send Him during the Roman reign.

When the Babylonians, the Medes and Persians and the Grecians wanted to take over a foreign land, they attacked it with force, decimated the cities, and destroyed the armies. They would then take selected men, as well as the women and children, and carry them back to their own kingdoms as slaves, leaving in their wake a desolate landscape. This very thing happened to the Israelites during the reign of the Babylonians. The Romans, however, had a very different strategy.

What the Romans did when they conquered foreign lands has come to be called *colonialism* or *imperialism*. They are really one and the same. *Imperialism* means "the extension of political power over territories that have been conquered," and since these conquered territories are called "colonies," the term colonialism also applies in this case.

Rome began as a small city-state, but gradually, by

force, it extended its control throughout the Mediterranean world. As it did, it colonized the surrounding areas. People were not deported from those areas. Instead they were taught Roman culture. Foreign lands were not, for the most part, devastated. Rather they were caused to prosper and that prosperity was used to further extend the Empire.

True, Rome saw to it that each colony was dependent upon the Motherland, but, at the same time, this was in the interest of each colony, since Rome was prosperous and Roman citizenship had many benefits.

True, Rome enforced colonization with the presence of Roman soldiers and appointed governors who were loyal to Rome more than to the locality. Yet, again, this had the benefit of bringing relative peace and calm to many areas, of opening up trade routes, and of extending the famous Roman highways.

Colonizers distributed their knowledge and culture throughout their sphere of influence, thus bringing improvement to the lives of many.

You can be sure that the Romans saw themselves as Liberators and as Benefactors of the people they ruled. This may not have been true in every single case, but in some cases, it was true. What is sure is that Rome knew how to transform the people of other nations into responsible Roman citizens. Instead of taking all the people back to Rome, they took Rome to the people.

Since taxes were collected in all the Roman colonies, Rome had a vested interest in the prosperity of each territory and did much to create a climate of economic growth and prosperity in each one.

Yes, Rome did rule with a rod of iron, as depicted in the dream of Nebuchadnezzar. Roman soldiers wasted no time in doing whatever was necessary to squash any uprising. They could be brutal. But their overlying philosophy was so different from other conquerors that we must admire them.

The lands of the promise were treated no differently by the Romans than were the other areas they ruled. Pilate was the sixth Roman Procurator of Judah and Samaria, and after him came Felix, who was appointed by Emperor Claudius in AD 53.

Making Greek a universal language simplified trade and travel and foreign relations. Travel was made much easier by the expert road and bridge builders sent from Rome to unite every corner of the Empire. And people who attained to Roman citizenship had great freedoms to move about and visit other lands.

What I find so fascinating about all of this is that the Roman Empire discovered something so close to the goals and methods of the Kingdom of God. God has called us to colonize our world, to spread the culture and language and learning of our Kingdom to men and women everywhere.

Britain, which had been colonized by the Romans, centuries later came to appreciate the methods those ancients employed and to copy them wherever they ruled. And, as we have seen, their influence has been far-reaching and lasting, as well. I have been to the Caribbean and to South America and have been amazed to find there many of the British standards established long ago, and to see that they were the same as we were taught in southern Africa.

Without arguing the politics of colonization, we can safely say that it was a most effective way of influencing the daily lives of the people it touched.

Many things the Romans did in their colonies cannot be condoned, and many things the British did in their colonies cannot be condoned. So, please don't misunderstand me. I am just saying that colonization was a powerful forum for making drastic and positive changes in people's lives.

The fact that Jesus came during the Roman era is meaningful to me because it gave Him certain advantages, as far as travel and communications. The leaders of the early Church also took advantage of the colonial system that was in place then to reach out to people all over the world and influence them for Christ, turning the world upside down in just a few years time.

The early church did not expect the people of other lands to travel to Jerusalem to receive the Gospel. They took the Gospel out to the people, wherever they happened to be found. These are lessons that we must learn to effectively influence the people around us.

I came from an unchurched background and was the first in our family to be saved. The other members of my family thought I was just passing through some sort of "fad" and that I would eventually come to my senses. I remember "preaching" to my parents and telling them that they were on their way to hell if they did not repent. That approach was not very much appreciated — as you can imagine.

I decided to stop preaching at them and just let them see my walk with the Lord. This approach soon bore fruit. It was not long before my mother's heart was touched, and I had the privilege of praying the sinner's prayer with her.

My older brother was next to receive Christ, and then came my older-middle sister. It took many years to reach my father, but just before he died I was able to pray with him and anoint him with oil. The tears in his eyes let me know that he had made a commitment to the Lord Jesus.

Finally, at fifty, my oldest sister received Christ into her life. It was not through me, but I believe the seeds of her salvation were sown in the first year of my conversion.

Noline and I are serving the Lord with all our hearts, as are our three children and our son-in-law. God promised that our whole household would be saved, and He has done it.

> *The time is fulfilled and the Kingdom of God is at hand: Repent ye, and believe the gospel.*
>
> Mark 1:15

The word translated *"time"* here is different from the *"time"* we saw in Galatians 4:4. The Greek word here is *kairos*, meaning "epoch; great and significant change." When Jesus taught about the Kingdom, He said that its coming would be a *kairos*, or life-changing, time and that those who repented and believed the Gospel would have their lives turned upside down.

Starting Now to Colonize Your World For Christ

When He linked the power of the message of the Gospel He preached with the powerful system of colonization the Romans had put into place, it was a recipe for explosive church growth, a powerful medium with which to reach the entire known world.

The Apostle Paul was a beneficiary of the colonization of Rome, since it gave him Roman citizenship and all the benefits that signified. Although he was a Jew, he was deeply influenced by the Romans and their lifestyle, and that influence was seen in his bold preaching. He believed in influencing people everywhere he went and changing their lives. One example can be seen when he and Silas were imprisoned in Philippi, and their jailor was moved by their faith and by the power of God that had set them free. When he asked what he could do to be saved, Paul said to him:

> *Believe in the Lord Jesus, and you will be saved —*
> *you and your household.*   Acts 16:31

Paul believed in the power of God to colonize an entire home for Christ. This is *"the power of God for the salvation of everyone who believes"*:

> *I am not ashamed of the gospel, because it is the*
> *power of God for the salvation of everyone who be-*
> *lieves: first for the Jew, then for the Gentile.*
>   Romans 1:16

The church has done a disservice to evangelism by referring to the building where we meet to worship as "the church." It's not. The people are the church, not the building. Another disservice is to make people believe that they must go to a church in order to be saved. These wrong concepts have influenced our thinking so much that they have robbed us of our ability to go forth and colonize the world with the Gospel. Just as soon as we have made a convert, we feel the need to deport them to another country, so to speak, by making them believe that the church is the building where they congregate and that nothing can be done outside that building.

I am not opposed to meeting in specific buildings. I believe we should gather to celebrate. But the amazing growth of the first-century church was due, not to the eloquence of the meeting places or to the oratory talents of a few gifted speakers, but because all new converts were taught to colonize their homes, and their neighbors' homes, and their relatives' homes, and their friends' homes with the Gospel of Christ.

The early church members not only met in large groups, they met from house to house. In groups of all sizes, they broke bread together, studied the apostles' teachings together, and prayed together. For them, the home was not just another place to meet. It was a place to be colonized so that old pagan influences could be broken and new heavenly influences could dominate.

When do you know that a home has been colonized? A truly colonized home is one where Jesus is Lord and Master, where the Bible is the accepted rule of life, and where believers, old and young alike, strengthen and help each other to make the transition from the ways of the world to the methods of God's Kingdom.

Every man and woman alive today deserves to hear this message. Jesus said:

> *Go ye into all the world, and preach the gospel to every creature.* Mark 16:15

Start colonizing your home for Christ, and start colonizing your world for Christ. Start breaking loose and taking your marriage to a higher level of fulfillment. Then, teach others these biblical principles.

CHAPTER THIRTEEN

TAKING YOUR RIGHTFUL PLACE IN GOD'S ECONOMY

Therefore let us leave the elementary teachings about Christ and go on to maturity, not laying again the foundation of repentance from acts that lead to death, and of faith in God, instruction about baptisms, the laying on of hands, the resurrection of the dead, and eternal judgment.　　　Hebrews 6:1-2

The first couple, Adam and Eve, were created by God and, although they were dependent on Him, they had freedom to live their lives as they desired. God provided a marvelous setting for them, and their daily activities revolved around that beautiful garden and around their fellowship with the Creator.

God didn't want robots who would mindlessly do His bidding, and Adam and Eve began their lives loving God of their own volition. How tragic that they chose, later, to listen to Satan's lies and, thus, fell.

God was not daunted by man's failure and disobedience to Him. He is a God of reconciliation and, since He knew all things from the beginning, His Son Jesus was already *"the Lamb slain from the foundation of the world."*

God had a plan of redemption for the family. This plan unfolded through the union of a man and a woman.

When God spoke to Abraham and told him to leave pagan Ur and take his wife Sarah to another land, a land God would show them, He gave Abraham a promise — that his seed would bless all the nations of the world. It was from the seed of Abraham that the Messiah was to come. Thus, God chose marriage and family as the vehicle for bringing redemption back into the world.

From that one couple, Abraham and Sarah, God brought forth an entire nation, the people of Israel, through whom the seed of salvation would come. God could have taken an existing nation, brought them under His covering, and used them for His purposes; but He chose not to do it that way. He took one man and one woman, formed of them a family, and of their family, a nation of destiny. The nation of Israel was raised up by God to demonstrate to the rest of the world a lifestyle pleasing to Him, as it was to bring forth the Savior of all mankind.

The good news for us today is that God is still able to take one man and one woman and, from them, raise up generations of God-fearing people. Just as He did in the past, so He will do again. And if we are willing to be the couple through which God can work, He will change our lives and use us to change countless others. We must make the transition, however, from the kingdom of the world to the Kingdom of God. We must break loose from the old and truly embrace the new.

Life was not always easy for the people of Israel, but even in their times of difficulty God kept His hand on them, guiding them, protecting them, and providing for them. Even when they were in Egypt, and in the wilderness, His provision was sure. That was a particularly trying time for the nation.

After Abraham and Sarah had died, during the time of their grandson Jacob, seventy-two family members moved to Egypt. What happened in Egypt was a tragedy of the highest degree. In a period of a few hundred years, the family went from being a prosperous and free nation to one that was enslaved and oppressed by the Egyptians. But when God's family cried out to Him for deliverance, He heard them and responded:

> *The LORD said, "I have indeed seen the misery of my people in Egypt. I have heard them crying out because of their slave drivers, and I am concerned about their suffering. So I have come down to rescue them from the hand of the Egyptians and to bring them up out of that land into a good and spacious land, a land flowing with milk and honey — the home of the Canaanites, Hittites, Amorites, Perizzites, Hivites and Jebusites. And now the cry of the Israelites has reached me, and I have seen the way the Egyptians are oppressing them. So now, go. I am sending you to Pharaoh to bring my people the Israelites out of Egypt."* Exodus 3:7-10

The rescue of the Israelites from the hands of their oppressors affected every area of their lives. Politically, they were saved from the tyranny of a foreign, autocratic, and oppressive power. Socially, they were rescued from the intolerable interference that the Egyptians were exercising over their family life. Economically, they were delivered from the burden of being forced into slave labor. And, spiritually, God rescued them from the realm of foreign gods and brought them into a place of freedom of unhindered worship of their Creator, and into a renewed covenant relationship with Him.

God wants to do the same thing for us today. We have become just as enslaved as the Israelites and God wants to set us free, in every sense of the word. The spiritual environment in which we live in the closing years of this century is every bit as polluted as that of Egypt, and its power has enslaved and used our children and friends. It is time to break loose.

When the people of God cried out to Him, He not only freed them from Egypt, but He took them toward the land He had promised to Abraham. When they approached the land of promise, however, these newly-delivered people found that they were in no condition to inherit the land. It was already occupied, and the occupants happened to be fierce giants. God had a purpose in that, as well. He wanted the people to grow in faith by facing the giants, dispossessing them, and taking back what rightfully belonged to them.

It did not sound easy at all to these freed slaves, and their mindset rendered them incapable of conquering the land. To possess the promise of God, they would have to face giants and pull down strong cities, and they were just not ready for that. Slavery had kept them small in their thinking and in their faith in God. It would take many more years in the wilderness before a new generation would take over and dare to attempt the conquest of the land.

I find the family of God so like this today. Because we have been enslaved by this world's thinking, we don't really know what we can do or what opportunities await us. Never in the history of this world have we seen such a concerted attack against the family and such resultant destruction. It looks like that runaway freight train has plowed right through the center of a lot of homes, leaving them totally devastated.

Will it take forty years for us to recover? Let's hope not; for there is much to possess, and time is short. Let us quickly leave behind our immature ways. Paul wrote:

> *What I am saying is that as long as the heir is a child, he is no different from a slave, although he owns the whole estate. He is subject to guardians and trustees until the time set by his father. So also, when we were children, we were in slavery under the basic principles of the world. But when the time had fully come, God sent his Son, born of a woman, born under law, to redeem those under law, that we might receive the full rights of sons. Because you are sons, God sent the Spirit of his Son into our hearts, the Spirit who calls out, "Abba, Father." So you are no longer a slave, but a son; and since you are a son, God has made you also an heir.*   Galatians 4:1-7

As long as an heir remains a child, Paul explained, he is not much different from a servant. He may actually own the entire estate, but he cannot handle it until he is mature enough, or in lawyerly terms, "of legal age."

Of course, Paul was not teaching the church about legal issues. He was saying that in order to inherit the fullness that God has for us, we must move on to spiritual maturity. We need to grow up. Our thinking must change. We must put off our childish ways and adopt a more mature sense of what is important in life. Children have no ability to make important decisions or important choices. They are lacking in maturity.

The land of promise lay before the children of Israel for many years. All they had to do was cross over Jordan and possess it. But after the spies had come back and reported the presence of giants in the land, few of the children of Abraham could grasp the fact that they were well able to do what God had commanded. So the land remained just beyond their grasp.

If we remain immature in our concepts of marriage, how can God give us His best? If we never learn the meaning of covenant and the meaning of the one-flesh relationship, how can we go beyond our present level of fulfillment?

Before His people would be ready to move forward and take the land promised to them, God had to act as both Father and Mother to them in the wilderness. As Father, He gave them His principles, and as Mother, He showed them His presence.

The principles had begun to come at Mt. Sinai, with the Ten Commandments, but there Moses received many other principles needed for the future growth and prosperity of the people in the land. God revealed Himself as

Taking Your Rightful Place In God's Economy

Mother through the wilderness Tabernacle, where He manifested to them His abiding and nurturing presence.

Moses' meeting with God at Mt. Sinai and the subsequent building of the wilderness Tabernacle were not just interesting additions to the life of the nation. These were God's way of bringing maturity to His people, of erasing the effects of so many years of abuse and neglect and of showing them His ways.

God's principles, when adhered to, produce maturity in every believer. God's presence, when enjoyed, produces the nurturing of knowing that we are loved. We need more of it, as married couples, if we are to come into the full stature and maturity of what God intended.

Every marriage needs principles by which to steer itself, and God's principles are unmatched because He is the architect of marriage. Every marriage deserves to be blessed by God's presence from its inception, for it is only when marriages are nurtured by His caring love that they take on a sense of genuine security. Far too many couples only experience the presence of God when they go into a church building, when God wants every family to bring His presence right into their homes. Without His nurturing care, any family can become dysfunctional.

There is absolutely no shortcut to maturity. It took forty years for the Israelites to get ready to conquer their promised land. In the meantime, they kept going in circles in the wilderness.

When forty years had passed, many of those who had been destined to possess the land had, sadly, died in the wilderness. They were never able to make the transition in their thinking. However, God had raised up a new

167

generation and had given them purpose. This is important, for maturity means nothing if you have no purpose in life. It would be like a weight-lifter who spent long hours in a gymnasium developing his muscles and then did nothing with them. Maturity is not just for show. It is not just so that we can say, "Hey, look at me. I'm all grown up." There is a purpose, a divine and eternal purpose, possessing all that God has prepared for us.

Rise up and take your rightful place in the economy of God. Break loose from the former mentality that is hindering you and move forward, taking your marriage to a higher level of fulfillment.

Chapter Fourteen

Working At It

The LORD God took the man and put him in the Garden of Eden TO WORK it and take care of it.

Genesis 2:15

It takes work to accomplish anything meaningful in life, and having a blessed marriage is no exception. Part of the maturity we seek is a sense of willingness to work for what we find worthwhile.

When our son Daryk graduated from high school, he was thinking to go right on to college, but, as his parents, we sensed that he didn't have the maturity to handle college just yet. When he mentioned going into the army reserves, we felt that this was a right and godly decision which would help him come into maturity in other areas of his life.

Once he had done his basic training and had returned home, he was kind of sitting around the house just waiting for the new semester of college to start, but that was still several months away. So I said to him one day, "Son, you cannot just sit around the house and wait for college. You have to go out and work."

The idea seemed shocking to him, at first. Didn't we want him any more? Why did he have to go out and hunt for work? But, in the end, the whole experience proved very helpful to him. When he applied for work in a local bank, he was not only accepted for a full-time position, he was told that if he needed financial assistance with his studies, the bank would help him.

We were pleased when he told us the news. After all, isn't this every parent's desire — to see their children mature to the place that they are serving a useful purpose in society? We are willing to raise our children and to fully support them, but only up to a point. We expect them to come to the place that they can leave home and find their own way in life. Some take longer than others to accomplish it, but if a child never comes to this point, we worry about them, and rightfully so. Work is the natural order of things.

If we have the necessary maturity, we will not mind the fact that it takes work for any couple to break down the old mindset of singleness and other damaging worldly concepts of marriage and be able to see ourselves as *"one flesh,"* a team, building a relationship together. God is searching for such mature individuals today, for He has great opportunities in His Kingdom for couples which are willing to truly become *"one flesh"* as He intended. Only the mature need apply, only those who are willing to work at it.

God set the pattern for us Himself. He worked:

> *By the seventh day God had finished the WORK he had been doing; so on the seventh day he rested from all his WORK.*   Genesis 2:2

When God created the first man and the first woman,

170

Working At It

He gave them a pattern for life and that pattern included work. He placed Adam and Eve over the Garden of Eden to *"take care of it."*

After Adam and Eve disobeyed God and ate of the forbidden fruit, something about work changed. Until then, their work had been always pleasant and enjoyable. Now they were forced to earn their bread *"by the sweat of [their] brow"* (Genesis 3:19). Still man was called to work, to *"do"*:

> *Do not let this Book of the Law depart from your mouth; meditate on it day and night, so that you may be careful to DO everything written in it. Then you will be prosperous and successful.* Joshua 1:8

Moses admonished Joshua to be careful to *do* all that was written in the book of the Law. Only then, only when his faith was accompanied by works, would he be prosperous and successful wherever he decided to place his foot.

The dignity and necessity of work was one of the major themes of the wisdom of Solomon in Ecclesiastes. A few examples:

> *A man can do nothing better than to eat and drink and find satisfaction in his WORK. This too, I see, is from the hand of God.* Ecclesiastes 2:24

> *I know that there is nothing better for men than to be happy and DO good while they live. That everyone*

171

*may eat and drink, and find satisfaction in all his
TOIL — this is the gift of God.*

Ecclesiastes 3:12-13

*So I commend the enjoyment of life, because nothing
is better for a man under the sun than to eat and
drink and be glad. Then joy will accompany him in
his WORK all the days of the life God has given him
under the sun.*   Ecclesiastes 8:15

*Go, eat your food with gladness, and drink your
wine with a joyful heart, for it is now that God favors what you DO.*   Ecclesiastes 9:7

A man should find satisfaction in his work. It is the gift
of God. When something costs us a little sweat, therefore,
let us not despise it, as is common today. Let us be grate-
ful for it.

We are *"God's workmanship"* and were created *"to do
good works"*:

*For we are God's WORKMANSHIP, created in
Christ Jesus to DO good WORKS, which God prepared in advance for us to DO.*   Ephesians 2:10

Our purpose in life, the work that we are chosen to do,
is prepared for us *"in advance."* Many people never discover their calling in life, partly because they have
remained infantile in their relationship with one another
and with God. More, however, have come to despise anything that takes effort. We have chosen, rather, the easy

path in life. And this is sad, because we are missing many of life's best blessings as a result of our wrong understanding of the purpose of work.

Jesus commanded us to work, as He had worked:

> *I tell you the truth, anyone who has faith in me will DO what I have been doing. He will DO even greater things than these, because I am going to the Father.*   John 14:12

He placed ministers in the Church, apostles, prophets, evangelists, pastors, and teachers, *"for the WORK of the ministry"* (Ephesians 4:11-12, KJV). Still we have millions of couples sitting on our church pews who are doing nothing. We need to put them to WORK.

When James wrote his letter to the churches, he showed that he preferred to show his faith by what he DID than simply by what he said (see James 2:14-26). It was James who showed us most emphatically that *"faith without WORKS is dead"* (James 2:20 and 26).

In fact the Bible teaches that a man is *"worse than an infidel"* (an unbeliever) if he refuses to work and provide for his family (1 Timothy 5:8) and that if a man refuses to work, he should not be allowed to eat (2 Thessalonians 3:10).

Satan has launched a concerted attack against humanity, doing everything he can to destroy the work ethic, doing everything he can to rob us of the time and the energy and the motivation to work at the things we all know to be vitally important to our lives. And, if he can keep us from working at something, he has gained the victory.

173

Working at your relationship can only help you spiritually. If we can get our relationships right, faith will grow alongside the relationship. It can only increase faith when you honor your spouse. It can only increase faith when you become a doer of the Word. In these last days it will be imperative that we, as Christians, have increased faith that God will be with us and will work through us in an unsaved world. Now is the time to put into practice that which God has given you, that faith may grow and increase in your heart and lives, and that your children may have a chance of living victoriously in their generation because of your obedience.

Our present world, and, sadly, even the Christian world, is void of good examples of one-flesh couples working together for common goals. In public ministries, for instance, we most often find the man acting as "the mighty man of God," and the wife being his faithful sidekick. Sometimes it is the other way around. Not many couples are joining their strengths to accomplish something meaningful and lasting for their families and for their God. This must change.

As more and more couples are willing to mature in their relationship with each other and with God, more of them will be released to do a special work for the Lord, and we will have more role models that we can look to, couples who are ministering together in the Body.

Noline and I have made a commitment to the Lord that wherever we go and minister, whether in a seminar or in a church service, we will minister together, as husband and wife. Only on very rare occasions have I had to go somewhere and minister by myself. Even though I was the pastor of three churches for more than eleven years and preached hundreds of sermons by myself, I have chosen not to minister singularly again. Both Noline and I feel it is tremendously important that we represent to the Body of Christ a role model of a one-flesh relationship.

This has not been an easy decision for either of us. For my part, it would be far easier to prepare a message to preach or teach on my own. Doing it together actually takes a lot longer.

Because the two of us think so differently, it sometimes takes hours for us to blend our thoughts together in such a way that we can both flow in the anointing and present what God wants. Still, we remain committed to that task, and together we go over and over the material in prayer until we have it in our hearts and spirits.

This book is very much a cooperative effort. Although my name appears on the title page, we wrote it together.

As far as public ministry is concerned, Noline is such an introvert that if she could, she would escape from public ministry altogether.

Once, when we were preparing to speak at a marriage retreat, Noline asked me to spend some more time with her going over our notes. I said, "You should have them already in your heart." With this, she burst into tears. So what was I to do at this point? Should I release her from speaking that day? Should I go over the notes with her again? Or should I just let her work through her feelings by herself? These thoughts went through my mind in a split second. I knew what was right. We prayed together, then we went back over the notes again until she felt confident.

It was only after the meeting that day that Noline opened her heart to me and told me what had been going on inside. She had been fighting the desire to back out of her commitment to teach with me. She resented the fact that she felt locked into the engagements I was booking, so she was purposely not going over the notes when she had time and leaving the matter for the last minute. That is why things had suddenly blown up. Her confession gave us the opportunity to pray through our feelings and find God's perfect will for us as a couple.

We both realize that the Body of Christ is in need of real life examples of men and woman who are willing to allow the presence of God to nurture their marriages and for God's principles to bring us into maturity so that we can do the work of the Lord in an effective manner. And we are both willing for God to use us in that way.

Just as every individual has a personal destiny, every marriage has a predetermined purpose in God. This is why God wants men and women to move beyond the born-again experience and find their proper place of service in the Kingdom of God.

And we must be willing to pay any cost. Maybe you've heard the saying, "We spend thousands on a wedding, hundreds on a divorce, and nothing on a marriage." Although the figures may have changed in the nineties, and we now spend more, this statement is still true for far too many Christian couples. We just don't invest time in our relationships.

With our finances, we are much more cautious. We join some sort of retirement plan that forces us to save money for the future. But when it comes to our marriage, we

Working At It

wait until we have completely burned out and are facing imminent divorce before we get serious about making the investments that would enable our marriage to stay strong through the rainy days.

Noline and I have made a long-term commitment to God to focus on His purpose for our lives as a couple and to be a role model for our children and our community. In doing so, we have learned a lot, experienced a lot, shared a lot, and been able, in the process, to take our marriage to a new level of fulfillment. We pray that, with God's help, you, the reader, may accomplish the same.

MMI Items That Will Bless Your Marriage

— Books by Neil and Noline Rhodes —

Breaking Loose: Taking Your Marriage to A Higher Level of Fulfillment

Why are so many Christian marriages being destroyed? What is holding God's people back from the deeper fulfillment He intended for our marriages? Neil Rhodes puts forth the forceful argument that we have been wrongly conditioned by this world's way of thinking and that we need to develop a whole new way of thinking, God's way of thinking, before we can experience the joys He intended for marriage.
B-16 .... $9.00

Refilling the Jars: Finding Hope After Adultery

Is there hope for a marriage when one of the partners has fallen into adultery and betrayed his or her spouse? Can Christians be forgiven the sin of adultery? Answers to these questions are never easy, but Neil and Noline Rhodes face them head on and present practical steps that can be taken to resolve the underlying marital conflicts that often lead to adulterous relationships.
B-15 .... $7.00

— Tapes by Neil and Noline Rhodes —

They Have No Wine (Love), 1 tape $4.00
One Flesh 1 tapes $4.00
Intimacy, 2 tapes $8.00
Highlights, 1 tape $4.00
5-TAPE SET **$16.00**

The Snare of the Fowler, *1 tape* $4.00
Dealing With Anger, *1 tape* $4.00
Fighting For the Home, *1 tape* $4.00
The Greatest Investment, *1 tape* $4.00
4-TAPE SET **$12.00**

Building Marriages Jesus Style,*1 tape* $4.00
The Kingdom and Relationships, *1 tape* ... $4.00
The Kingdom and Influence, *1 tape* $4.00
The Kingdom and Righteousness, Peace and
Joy in Marriage, *1 tape* $4.00
4-TAPE SET **$12.00**

Unity of the Spirit in the Home, *1 tape* $4.00
Unity of the Faith,*1 tape* $4.00
Unity in Relationships, *1 tape* $4.00
Unity in Communion, *1 tape* $4.00
4-TAPE SET **$12.00**

TO ORDER, CALL (303) 933-3331 or FAX (303) 933-2153

— OTHER BOOKS —

Whose Report Will You Believe?
Marilyn Phillipps

In this book, Marilyn Phillipps recounts the expectations, crisis and moments of lonely helplessness from her own courtship and marriage against a backdrop of God's power and covenant faithfulness. An encouragement to those who are fighting for their marriage, without cooperation from their spouse. Available in English and Spanish

B-09 .... $3.00

First Aid For A Wounded Marriage, *Marilyn Phillipps*

A booklet designed to minister to those whose marriage is troubled and those believing for the healing of their marriage and their spouse. Available in English and Spanish.

B-01 .... $2.00

Eyes of Faith, *Carol O'Hara*

Through her own honesty and transparency, Carol O'Hara teaches how to see people and circumstances as God sees them.

B-10 .... $2.00

Marriage: Covenant or Contract, *Craig Hill*

A comprehensive study of marriage, divorce, and remarriage in the church. Learn what the Word really says.

B-06 .... $3.00

Help! My Spouse Wants Out, *Craig Hill*

Practical advice for those with serious marriage difficulties.

B-13 .... $8.00

An Alternative To Divorce, *Marilyn Conrad*

The biblical alternative to divorce. Includes scriptural guidelines for marriage healing.

B-02 .... $2.00

Standing Day By Day

Daily prayer journal and diary for those who are standing for their marriage. (Covers 3 months.)

B-11 .... $7.00

Together, Day By Day

Daily prayer journal and diary for couples to record special things the Lord has shared with them. (Covers 3 months.)

B-12 .... $7.00

TO ORDER, CALL MMI: (303) 933-3331
FAX: (303) 933-2153

— OTHER TAPES —

Keys to Marriage Healing and Growth, *Mike & Marilyn Phillipps*

A 6-tape series that includes their testimony, steps to soul healing, sexual healing, and family healing.

T-6-KMH00 .... $24.00

Understanding One-Flesh, *Mike & Marilyn Phillipps*

A 2-tape series that shares God's blueprint for covenant and the one-flesh vision.

T-2-UOF00 .... $10.00

Rebuilding the City Wall, *Craig Hill, Neil & Noline Rhodes, Mike & Marilyn Phillipps*

From the MMI '91 Convention. Based on Nehemiah. A powerful 3-tape series on the restoration of marriage and family. Learn what the wall is and why it must be rebuilt in this hour.

T-3-RCW00 .... $12.00

The Third Season, *Mike & Marilyn Phillipps*

A 3-tape series based on Isaiah 37:30, examining the time to receive and the time to give. Discover your season.

T-3-TS00 .... $12.00

First Aid Kit For A Wounded Marriage, *Mike & Marilyn Phillipps*

A 4-tape series which includes a marriage version of the familiar household first aid kit that families run to when someone is hurt. Recognizably packaged kit contains: "First Aid For A Wounded Marriage," "Whose Report Will You Believe?" Mike & Marilyn's testimony tapes, plus actual "scripture BandAids."

T-2-FA00 .... $16.00

— POWERHOUSE APPAREL —

Married For Life Sweatshirts

Embroidered MMI logo on 12 oz. athletic cut. (Available colors: Ash with navy lettering, black with silver lettering, navy with gold lettering, and white with black lettering.) (Available sizes: M, L, XL, and XXL.) Specify color and size when ordering.

C-SS-MFL $30.00

Married For Life T-Shirts

Embroidered MMI logo on heavyweight cotton t-shirts. (Available colors: Ash with navy lettering, black with silver lettering, navy with gold lettering, and white with black lettering.) (Available sizes: M, L, XL, and XXL.) Specify color and size when ordering.

C-TS-MFL $20.00

TO ORDER, CALL MMI: (303) 933-3331
FAX: (303) 933-2153

Ministry address:

Marriage Ministries International
P.O. Box 1040
Littleton, Colorado 80160-1040

PHONE: (303) 730-3333
FAX: (303) 798-5057
E-mail: Neil@marriage.org